The Case for Creativity

The Case for Creativity

*Two decades' evidence of the link between
imaginative marketing and commercial success.*

James Hurman

AUT MEDIA

Published by AUT Media
P. O. Box 7125 Wellesley St
AUCKLAND
www.aut.ac.nz
Email: info@tangiblemedia.co.nz

Copyright © James Hurman 2011
First published 2011

The author has asserted his moral rights in the work.

This book is copyright. Except for the purposes of fair reviewing, no part of this publication (whether it be in any eBook, digital, electronic or traditionally printed format or otherwise) may be reproduced or transmitted in any form or by any means, electronic, digital or mechanical, including CD, DVD, eBook, PDF format, photocopying, recording, or any information storage and retrieval system, including by any means via the internet or World Wide Web, or by any means yet undiscovered, without permission in writing from the publisher. Infringers of copyright render themselves liable to prosecution.

ISBN 978-0-9582997-3-2

Layout by Shayna Armstrong

Edited by Veronica de Lautour

Contents

Chapter One: The case for this book	9
Chapter Two: The case for creative agencies	23
Chapter Three: Identifying creativity	41
Chapter Four: The case for originality	55
Chapter Five: The case for creative advertising (according to Donald Gunn, the IPA and McKinsey & Company)	77
Chapter Six: How creativity makes advertising more effective (according to Bill Bernbach and a tweed of academics)	99
Chapter Seven: The case for creative companies	109
Chapter Eight: The future case for creativity	127
Chapter Nine: The case for creativity	151
Appendix: The 15 studies	166
Notes	172

1. The case for this book

"Nobody reads advertising. People read what interests them, and sometimes it's an ad."

Howard Luck Gossage
Gossage, Freeman & Partners, San Francisco, 1950s

The case for this book

In 2009 a pair of advertising creatives from Australia set out to resolve one of their industry's oldest uncertainties: Does creativity make advertising more effective?

Ben Couzens and Jim Ingram chose an ordinary product – a BMX bike for sale on eBay. It had an ordinary ad: 'Up for sale is a reliance boomerang BMX. Quite rare. Some rust on forks and bars. Pick up only from Clayton. Happy Bidding.'

They bought that ordinary BMX for the ordinary price of $27.50. Then they conducted an experiment in which they sold the exact same product in the exact same medium, but this time added creativity.

Their ad went like this:[1]

BMX Super Rad Extreme 2000

This is a max wicked sick BMX.

It's a Reliance Boomerang and it's done heaps of maximum extreme stunts. I have mostly done stunts on this bike since forever. Once I did a boom gnarly stunt trick and a girl got pregnant just by watching my extremeness to the maxxxx.

Some details about sickmax BMX:

Comes with everything you see including:

TOPS AS SUSPENSION REAR FORKS!! 2 x wheels. 1 x seat. I will even throw in my sick BMXing name for FREE – Wicked Styx.

Has minor surface rust on handlebars and front forks (easily removed). More rust on rear forks (as shown in pics). Tyres hold air but are pretty old.

Basically, it's an old BMX, but its radness is still 100% intact.

Tricks I have done on this BMX:

Endos – 234

Sick Wheelies – 687

Skids – 143,000

Bunny Hops – 2 (Bunny Hops are gay and my brother dared me to do them, which I did because I'm Rad to the power of Sick.)

Flipouts – 28

Basically if you buy this bike you will become a member to every club that was ever invented, worldwide, because you will be awesome.

The case for this book

Couzens & Ingram's Wicked Sick BMX

On day one the bids reached $55, double what had been paid for the bike. Dozens of enquiries came in. "How long are the skids that this bike can do?" asked one bidder. "The skids odometer shows 128,992 metres," Ben replied, "but once I did a skid that went for two weeks."

On day two there were numerous blog posts with titles like 'one of the best eBay ads I've ever seen'.

By day three the ad's copy had made its way into the Australian vernacular. "This apple fritter is rad to the power of sick!" tweeted a twitterer midway through his snack. "JP O'Brien once did a bmx skid that went for two weeks," boasted JP O'Brien on Facebook.

The bike finally sold for $134.50 – nearly five times the previous sale value of the product – demonstrating the value of creativity, at least to selling BMX bikes on eBay.

Much has been said about the need for creativity in advertising. Perhaps the most lucid advice is Bill Bernbach's timeless observation that "if your advertising goes unnoticed, everything else is academic".

And let's be honest, quite a lot of advertising goes unnoticed. Consider your last 24 hours. You will have been exposed to countless ads. In 2007, Yankelovich Research estimated that city dwellers were exposed to over 3,000 commercial messages a day.[2] How many can you recall right now? One percent? That's 30. Go on, have a try.

Harvard University research shows that, of the thousands of ads that marketers pay for us to be exposed to each day, we're oblivious to all but 76. And it isn't that we actively choose not to engage with the rest – rather our subconscious filters them out so effectively that we're completely unaware of them. Then, of the 76 ads that make it through, just 12 make any sort of impression on us. And finally, of those 12, it's unusual for us to be able to recall more than two of them the next day.[3]

American businessman John Wanamaker famously said, "I know that half of my advertising dollars are wasted... I just don't know which half." If Harvard and Yankelovich are right, we're wasting somewhat more than half our advertising dollars.

So why does so much advertising go unnoticed?

"Nobody reads advertising," said Howard Gossage, 1950s San Francisco adman. "People read what interests them, and sometimes it's an ad."

The classic case for creativity is that it's something of a Trojan horse. It takes a marketing message and wraps it up in an idea interesting enough to avoid going unnoticed. Interesting enough to stand out among a barrage of commercial messages too dense for any normal person to even begin to negotiate.

"This is a really nice idea," a senior client said to me recently. "I like it a lot. But it's getting in the way of the product message. We just need to clearly communicate that message."

It's easy to succumb to the belief that when consumers are

THE CASE FOR CREATIVITY

Some of the 3,000 commercial messages researchers estimate we're exposed to each day

distracted from what they're doing by an ad, they're in a state of 'paying attention'. That as long as we communicate a message clearly to them, they'll listen, learn, and buy.

Even the most conventional wisdom suggests this isn't the case. Yet as logical as the arguments for creativity are, scepticism is rife.

In 1995, academics published in the *Journal of Advertising Research* noted that "within the advertising industry, there seems to be a never-ending struggle between those who create the advertising ('creatives') and those advertising managers who insist that it be 'effective'."[4]

Their observation reflects a belief from some corners of our industry that creativity and effectiveness are two separate and unrelated outcomes. It's a belief held emphatically by some. In 2006 the marketing head of a major German FMCG company told McKinsey & Company that "creativity is irrelevant at best. Often, it is downright harmful to advertising success."[5]

The sceptical opinion is that creativity is a sort of irresponsible folly that advertising creatives attempt to get past unwitting clients in order to win awards. That creativity has little if anything to do with making advertising more effective. And that agencies that pursue highly creative ideas are quite knowingly sabotaging their clients' chances of success.

It's true that creative people are highly motivated by their own passion for creativity and the creative awards system that recognises their level of achievement among their peers. But is that really evidence in itself that they're working at cross-purposes to effectiveness?

For both creative people and their agencies, creative awards have a motivational capacity. They guide, often to a large extent, the kind of work agencies encourage their clients to produce. Those clients often harbour scepticism and regard creativity as a distraction from selling. And it's perfectly reasonable to expect clients to require us to address that scepticism, to expect us to let creativity be such a driver only if we can prove that it's *not* a distraction from selling.

If indeed more creative advertising is *less* effective, then the case rests. Our industry has engineered itself to work hopelessly toward two mutually exclusive outcomes, and we need to rethink the way we're incentivised.

But if more creative advertising is *more* effective, then the creative awards system is, in a way, a beneficial incentive scheme – one that cunningly uses fame and peer caché as a way to motivate agencies to produce more effective work for their clients.

Anecdotally, creative advertising does appear to punch above its weight.

According to the UK's Institute of Practitioners in

Advertising, approximately one in every 7,000 campaigns is creative enough to win a creative award.[6] In other words, barely any advertising is highly creative.

Statistically speaking this means that effectiveness awards, which usually have in the vicinity of a few dozen awarded campaigns, should have either zero, or at very best one, creatively-awarded campaign among their ranks.

In fact, if you look at your local Effies show you'll find that usually around a fifth of the winners also received creative awards. Look at the remainder and you'll tend to find that most of those campaigns, while not being creative award material, are more creative than the average campaign you see on television. That's a massive over-representation of creative campaigns at effectiveness award shows, suggesting that more creative advertising does indeed work harder.

Of course, that's a very unscientific observation.

And that's precisely the problem with the debate around creativity in advertising. It's based entirely on anecdotal evidence, piles of which exist on both sides of the debate.

Creative cynics will point to examples of creatively-awarded campaigns that haven't produced a business result, and to equally numerous examples of megabrands being built on what you'd consider uncreative marketing.

Those *for* creativity will use contrasting examples of creative award winners that have won major effectiveness accolades and point to highly creative challenger brands as evidence of the business potential of an original and colourful approach.

Both sides seem to have a point. What's been lacking, however, is a conclusion. As passionate as both sides are in their rhetoric, and as convinced as they are by their own small sets of personal experience and anecdotal examples, neither has been capable of showing whether or not more creative advertising is, statistically speaking, more effective.

We typically net out at a circular game of conjecture. Our industry agrees to disagree. And we forge ahead in slightly different directions.

"So many creatives tell me, 'I wish we could prove that great ads actually made a difference'," says Tess Alps, CEO of Thinkbox, the UK's marketing body for commercial broadcasters. "Creative awards are often derided by advertisers, who say 'oh it's just creative people awarding themselves at stupid self-indulgent ceremonies, it's got nothing to do with business'. Could we actually look at whether that was true or not? Is there a correlation between the sort of ads that gain awards and high levels of effectiveness?"[7] Alps was introducing the findings of a major study of creativity that we'll look at later, but the question that she's asked is the very one this book hopes to answer.

If we're after more effective advertising, should we pursue a more creative approach, or a more conservative one?

And can we answer that question with something sounder than isolated examples and conjecture? Can we compare, with significant data sets and academic methodologies, the more creative agencies and campaigns with the less creative ones, and measure the effectiveness of those two groups?

Can we determine, once and for all, whether it is better for advertisers to employ a more creative agency and encourage a more creative approach?

Is more creative advertising more effective advertising?

Let's find out.

THE CASE FOR CREATIVITY

2. The case for creative agencies

"Our objective is effectiveness. Our strategy is creativity."

Bartle Bogle Hegarty

In 2006 *Advertising Age* marveled at the $37 million they estimated Madison Avenue agencies would spend that year entering creative award programmes. "A number that looks like vanity gone wild," they said, "given that the pencils and lions are often denigrated as little more than ego-inflating devices for the creatives that crave them."[8]

The report went on to discover that the USA's six most creatively awarded agency networks – BBDO, DDB, TBWA\, Ogilvy, Wieden+Kennedy and Saatchi & Saatchi – were also the fastest-growing, suggesting that creative awards might just be as attractive to clients as they are to creative people.

But despite that ostensible evidence, it's a suggestion that tends to be rejected. Judy Neer, president of Pile & Co (a consultancy that manages client/agency relationships) told *Ad Age* that "our clients typically never care about award shows". Dick Roth, founder of similar company Roth Associates, agreed. "In making a new agency selection it is not a key criteria, at all," he

THE CASE FOR CREATIVITY

said. "Does winning awards influence new business decisions? I think not."

Across the Atlantic, Martin Jones of UK relationship consultancy AAR told *Campaign* an illuminating story. "I was once asked to look at the customer journey that a new-business prospect might make when visiting a new agency," he said. "'What do clients think about putting creative awards up in reception?' was the first question. Unfortunately, the agency chief was expecting a definitive answer. My response had to take into account the way in which clients post-rationalise their thoughts: If they've had a good meeting and like the people, they will think you care about your product. If they've had a poor meeting, they will simply see your display of creative awards as being a focus on art rather than commerce."[9]

It's an insightful commentary on human nature, but also brings to light the issue that we are without general agreement on whether there is any correlation between creative awards and effectiveness, leaving clients' views of creative awards to be based solely on their feelings about the people who've won them.

That we choose to weigh creativity and effectiveness in separate baskets is a quirk that often niggles even creative people.

"Everything that's wrong with the advertising business can be encapsulated by the fact that we have separate awards shows for creativity and effectiveness," said Deutsch L.A. Chief Creative Officer Eric Hirshberg to *Creativity* in 2008. "It's hard to imagine what the analogous award shows would be in other creative industries. It would be like the journalism industry giving out one award for prose, and another for accuracy."[10]

And yet as agreeable as Erics words are, in one sense at least we are fortunate to have evolved in such a peculiar way. The oddity of separate measurement systems for creativity and effectiveness has afforded us the ability to learn whether there's truly a relationship between them.

By 2008 data from creative and effectiveness award programmes had become not only comprehensive but widely available. The Gunn Report provided a list of the world's most creative agencies according to their performances at creative award shows. And the results of effectiveness shows such as the UK's IPA Effectiveness Awards and the USA's Effies were online for all to see. Nobody had compared the data sets at that point, but it didn't take more than a few quiet January mornings to punch them into a spreadsheet and see what happened.

The 2007 Gunn Report Top 50 featured exactly ten UK and ten USA agencies, which I used to build a set of 'most creative agencies' to compare against a set of 'less creative' agencies. The most creative set included perennial creative favourites like BBH and AMV BBDO in the UK, and Wieden+Kennedy and TBWA\ in the USA. The less creative set comprised the most successful agencies that hadn't made it into the 2007 Gunn Report – ten from the UK including McCann Erickson and VCCP, and ten from the USA including JWT and Ogilvy & Mather.

I then gathered together the effectiveness award performance of each agency. To build a picture of consistent effectiveness, as opposed to simply having had one good year, I totalled their performances from the most recent four effectiveness award shows.

What that analysis revealed was that the most creative agencies had won an average of 11.2 effectiveness awards over that period, whereas the less creative shops had won an average of 8.2. There wasn't a lot in it, really, and although the most creative shops seemed more effective on average, there were frequent anomalies such as the less creative JWT USA with 24 effectiveness awards, eclipsing the highly creative Goodby, Silverstein & Partners with just 11.

However, the fact of the matter is that agencies come in all shapes and sizes, and you'd expect that large agencies win more creative awards and more effectiveness awards simply because across a year they have more chances to produce award winning work.

So to get a true measure of effectiveness, I really needed to take agency size into account. After all, a huge agency winning 11 Effies is a very different thing from an agency a tenth of

2007 MOST CREATIVE UK & USA AGENCIES

	Revenue (US$M)	Effectiveness Awards Won	Effectiveness Awards Won per $100M Revenue
DDB (UK)	456	29	6.4
TBWA\ (UK)	301	9	3.0
Fallon (UK)	101	2	2.0
BBH (UK)	407	7	1.7
Lowe (UK)	360	6	1.7
Leo Burnett (UK)	366	6	1.6
AMV BBDO (UK)	752	8	1.1
Wieden+Kennedy (UK)	101	1	1.0
Saatchi & Saatchi (UK)	413	3	0.7
Mother (UK)	274	0	-
Fallon (USA)	62	19	30.6
Leo Burnett (USA)	312	39	12.5
Goodby, Silverstein & Partners	102	11	10.8
TBWA\ (USA)	199	19	9.5
DDB (USA)	278	25	9.0
Arnold (USA)	90	8	8.9
Wieden+Kennedy (USA)	76	6	7.9
BBDO (USA)	444	23	5.2
Crispin Porter + Bogusky (USA)	86	3	3.5
Cliff Freeman & Partners (USA)	12	0	-
AVERAGE	259.6	11.2	4.3

2007 LESS CREATIVE UK & USA AGENCIES

	Revenue (US$M)	Effectiveness Awards Won	Effectiveness Awards Won per $100M Revenue
DraftFCB (UK)	92	3	3.3
RKCR/Y&R (UK)	407	8	2.0
VCCP (UK)	182	3	1.6
WCRS (UK)	266	3	1.1
JWT (UK)	652	7	1.1
Grey (UK)	370	3	0.8
Publicis (UK)	554	3	0.5
M&C Saatchi (UK)	515	2	0.4
McCann Erickson (UK)	576	2	0.3
Ogilvy & Mather (UK)	521	0	-
McKinney (USA)	37	15	40.5
Ogilvy & Mather (USA)	290	23	7.9
Cramer-Krasselt (USA)	118	9	7.6
JWT (USA)	445	24	5.4
Publicis (USA)	208	10	4.8
Y&R (USA)	250	12	4.8
DraftFCB (USA)	210	10	4.8
McCann Erickson (USA)	443	17	3.8
Euro RSCG (USA)	182	5	2.7
Grey (USA)	236	5	2.1
AVERAGE	327.7	8.2	2.5
The Most Creative Agencies:	0.8 times as big	1.4 times as many Effectiveness Awards	1.7 times as many Effectiveness Awards per $100M

The 'Most Creative' agencies are those that appeared in the 2007 Gunn Report Top 50. The 'Less Creative' agencies are the best performing agencies not in the 2007 Gunn Report Top 50, based on revenue and effectiveness award performance. 'Revenue' is as reported in *Advertising Age* 2006 and *Campaign* 2005. 'Effectiveness Awards Won' is a total across the previous four USA Effies or IPA Effectiveness Awards respectively.

The case for creative agencies

their size winning eight.

Fortuitously, the billings information for all the agencies involved was also publicly available, and once I punched that data into my spreadsheet I found a much clearer picture.

The most creative agencies were on average 20% smaller than the less creative ones. Which meant that, per US$100 million billed, the most creative agencies had won 4.3 effectiveness awards, against the less creative agencies' 2.5.

The most creative agencies looked to be over 70% more efficient at creating highly effective work. And although upon crude analysis JWT USA had appeared to be a more effective agency than Goodby, Silverstein & Partners, a second look showed them to be over four times Goodby's size. JWT's resulting effectiveness was 5.4 Effies per US$100 million billed. Goodby's were twice as effective at 10.8.

The analysis provided a little solace for those working in highly creative agencies, and went some way toward disproving the theory that agencies that dominate creative awards do so at the cost of their clients' business success. In fact, it seemed to be quite the opposite.

Three years later the world had moved on. Many of the agencies in my original 'most creative' list had fallen from the Gunn Report's Top 50. And, conversely, agencies that had once lacked creative reputations were now the darlings of Cannes.

On top of that, looking back I could see flaws in my analysis. I had taken winners out of just one Gunn Report, as opposed to the agencies that had consistently, over time, maintained high levels of creativity. Similarly, my billings figures were from just one year. My 'less creative' list was a gut-feel group rather than having had any real selection criteria. And I'd included agencies that had won no effectiveness awards, and who may well have had an internal policy to abstain from entering those awards.

I was curious to see what would happen in 2011 if I looked at a much deeper and more current set of data. So again I took advantage of a few quiet January mornings.

This time I decided to look at all the data from a five-year period: 2006-2010. I'd add up all Gunn Report points, all effectiveness awards, and all billings for those five years.

For my list of 'most creative' agencies, I wanted only the consistently creative shops, rather than agencies that had made it into the Gunn Report's Top 50 off one lucky year. So I made a list of those agencies that had been included in the Gunn Report's Top 50 at least twice between 2006 and 2010.

Then, to create a comparison 'less creative' group, I took the agencies that had the largest billings 2006-2010, according to *Advertising Age* and *Campaign* magazine reports, and who either hadn't made it into the Gunn Report Top 50, or had featured only once.

Some agencies choose not to enter effectiveness awards,

and so to include them would confuse the data, as there's no way of telling how effective they would have been had they entered. So I included only agencies that had won at least one effectiveness award across the period – proof that they didn't have a policy against entering.

That left me with a group of 12 USA and six UK 'most creative' agencies, and a comparison group of 12 USA and six UK 'less creative' agencies:

Most Creative Agencies:

Arnold (USA)
BBDO (USA)
BBH (USA)
Crispin Porter + Bogusky (USA)
DDB (USA)
Goodby Silverstein & Partners (USA)
Grupo Gallegos (USA)
Leo Burnett (USA)
McCann Erickson (USA)
Saatchi & Saatchi (USA)
TBWA\ (USA)
Wieden+Kennedy (USA)
AMV BBDO (UK)
BBH (UK)
DDB (UK)
Fallon (UK)
Leo Burnett (UK)
Saatchi & Saatchi (UK)

Less Creative Agencies:

Campbell-Ewald (USA)
Deutsch (USA)
Doner (USA)
DraftFCB (USA)
Euro RSCG (USA)
Grey (USA)
Hill Holliday (USA)
JWT (USA)
Ogilvy Advertising (USA)
Publicis (USA)
Richards Group (USA)
Y&R (USA)
JWT (UK)
M&C Saatchi (UK)
McCann Erickson (UK)
Ogilvy Advertising (UK)
Publicis (UK)
Rainey Kelly Campbell Roalfe/Y&R (UK)

Next, I tallied the effectiveness award wins from 2006-2010 for each agency. The USA tallies came from the USA's Effie Awards and the UK tallies came from the UK's IPA Effectiveness Awards.

And a picture began to emerge.

The USA's most creative agencies averaged 13.3 Effies over the five-year period. The USA's less creative agencies averaged 8.2. The UK's most creative agencies averaged 4.7 IPA Effectiveness Awards over the five years (IPA awards being given out much more sparingly than Effies). The UK's less creative agencies averaged 4.0.

Overall, the most creative agencies had won 1.5 times as many effectiveness awards.

To bring more colour to the picture, I'd collected some extra data that I'd forgone in 2008. I'd noted the quality of the effectiveness awards – i.e. whether they were a Bronze, Silver, Gold, or 'Grand Effie' or 'IPA Grand Prix' – and then assigned a points system to those awards to show not only how many effectiveness awards an agency had won, but also the overall quality of those wins, giving each agency an 'effectiveness points' total for the period. A Bronze earned one point, a Silver two points, a Gold three points and a Grand four. This gave me a way to recognise the agencies that were truly the *most* effective.

With that data factored in, the most creative agencies proved even more effective – with an average of 1.7 times as many effectiveness points as their less creative counterparts.

2006-2010 MOST CREATIVE UK & USA AGENCIES

	Revenue (US$M)	Effectiveness Awards Won	Effectiveness Points	Effectiveness Awards Won per $1B Revenue	Effectiveness Points per $1B Revenue
Arnold (USA)	645.9	4	7	6.2	10.8
BBDO (USA)	2269.2	18	35	7.9	15.4
BBH (USA)	162.0	6	14	37.0	86.4
Crispin Porter + Bogusky (USA)	529.4	8	17	15.1	32.1
DDB (USA)	1385.2	35	70	25.3	50.5
Goodby Silverstein & Partners (USA)	427.0	19	45	44.5	105.4
Grupo Gallegos (USA)	40.4	1	1	24.8	24.8
Leo Burnett (USA)	1244.5	29	55	23.3	44.2
McCann Erickson (USA)	2348.4	7	13	3.0	5.5
Saatchi & Saatchi (USA)	1004.8	10	22	10.0	21.9
TBWA\ (USA)	964.5	12	28	12.4	29.0
Wieden+Kennedy (USA)	458.1	10	20	21.8	43.7
AMV BBDO (UK)	3098.2	6	14	1.9	4.5
BBH (UK)	1830.6	12	24	6.6	13.1
DDB (UK)	1425.3	4	7	2.8	4.9
Fallon (UK)	1060.3	2	5	1.9	4.7
Leo Burnett (UK)	1463.5	3	7	2.0	4.8
Saatchi & Saatchi (UK)	1342.4	1	2	0.7	1.5
USA MOST CREATIVE AVERAGE	956.6	13.3	27.3	19.3	39.1
UK MOST CREATIVE AVERAGE	1703.4	4.7	9.8	2.7	5.6
MOST CREATIVE AVERAGE	1205.5	10.4	21.4	13.7	28.0

2006-2010 LESS CREATIVE UK & USA AGENCIES

	Revenue (US$M)	Effectiveness Awards Won	Effectiveness Points	Effectiveness Awards Won per $1B Revenue	Effectiveness Points per $1B Revenue
Campbell-Ewald (USA)	979.5	5	9	5.1	9.2
Deutsch (USA)	738.0	7	13	9.5	17.6
Doner (USA)	789.0	3	7	3.8	8.9
DraftFCB (USA)	1637.3	3	12	1.8	7.3
Euro RSCG (USA)	1133.9	6	11	5.3	9.7
Grey (USA)	1130.0	11	20	9.7	17.7
Hill Holliday (USA)	694.3	1	2	1.4	2.9
JWT (USA)	1744.4	25	45	14.3	25.8
Ogilvy Advertising (USA)	1179.0	25	47	21.2	39.9
Publicis (USA)	868.3	5	8	5.8	9.2
Richards Group (USA)	810.5	2	2.5	6.2	29.0
Y&R (USA)	1394.0	5	10	3.6	7.2
JWT (UK)	2273.6	4	7	1.8	3.1
M&C Saatchi (UK)	1942.8	1	2	0.5	1.0
McCann Erickson (UK)	2217.9	3	4	1.4	1.8
Ogilvy Advertising (UK)	1676.7	5	6	3.0	3.6
Publicis (UK)	1667.4	1	1	0.6	0.6
RKCR/Y&R (UK)	1789.2	10	22	5.6	12.3
USA LESS CREATIVE AVERAGE	1091.5	8.2	15.8	7.0	13.5
UK LESS CREATIVE AVERAGE	1927.9	4.0	7.0	2.1	3.7
LESS CREATIVE AVERAGE	**1370.3**	**6.8**	**12.8**	**5.4**	**10.2**
The Most Creative Agencies:	**0.9**	**1.5**	**1.7**	**2.6**	**2.7**
	times as big	times as many Effectiveness Awards	times as many Effectiveness Points	times as many Effectiveness Awards per $1B	times as many Effectiveness Points per $1B

The 'Most Creative' agencies are those that have appeared in the Gunn Report Top 50 at least twice between 2006 and 2010. The 'Less Creative' agencies are the largest USA and UK agencies by billings that had won at least one Effectiveness Award between 2006 and 2010, and who either did not appear in the Gunn Report Top 50 between 2006 and 2010 or appeared only once. 'Revenue' is total revenue for the 2005-2009 years, as reported in industry journals Advertising Age (USA) and Campaign (UK). 'Effectiveness Points' are calculated as follows: 1 point for a Bronze, 2 points for a Silver, 3 points for a Gold and 4 points for a Grand Effie or IPA Grand Prix.

The case for creative agencies

Finally, I added in the billings information. Totalling revenue for the 2005-2009 financial years (the years when the work that was later awarded would have run), I found the most creative agencies to have been on average 10% smaller than the less creative ones.

By dividing the revenue by the number of effectiveness awards, I could calculate the true measure of an agency's effectiveness – how efficient they'd been at achieving effectiveness – measured by how many effectiveness awards, and effectiveness points, they'd won per $1 billion billed.

What the data show is that the USA's most creative agencies won an average of 19.3 Effies, and 39.1 effectiveness points, per $1 billion billed. Their less creative fellow Americans won just 7.0 Effies and 13.5 effectiveness points.

The UK's most creative agencies won an average of 2.7 IPA Effectiveness Awards, and 5.6 effectiveness points, per $1 billion billed. The less creative UK shops won just 2.1 IPA awards and 3.7 points.

What this revealed was that in terms of true overall effectiveness, the most creative shops were over two and a half times more effective. They'd won 2.6 times as many effectiveness awards and 2.7 times as many effectiveness points.

Creative ambition raises eyebrows not because the business world is against creativity per se, but rather because of the nervousness they feel that agencies will prioritise creativity over effectiveness. But is it really ever a case of prioritising one over the other?

BBH have concocted perhaps the most lucid explanation of the relationship between the two.

"Our objective is effectiveness," they say. "Our strategy is creativity."

At a guess I'd say their mantra resonates with creatively ambitious agencies everywhere. Rather than a case of one or the other being most important, creativity is simply the strategy to achieve effectiveness.

The numbers suggest it's working – which is unsurprising given business history has shown that the companies that truly live and breathe their strategies are the ones that most often achieve their objectives.

There is clearly a lot more to choosing an agency than simply checking how many awards they've won. In our business relationships are everything, and even the most effective agency is prone to producing poor results under the burden of an unhappy client partnership.

And of course, even in the more conclusive 2006-2010 study, there still exists a small handful of examples of extremely effective agencies that have gone without at creative award shows.

However, what these findings suggest is that, by and large, if an agency does well at creative award shows, it'll also be doing well in terms of effectiveness; that there is a much stronger correlation between high creativity and high effectiveness than there is between lower creativity and high effectiveness; and that if you see a ridiculous surfeit of pencils and lions in the reception area of an agency you're visiting, it's probably evidence of something more than just creativity.

3. Identifying creativity

THE CASE FOR CREATIVITY

"It's whatever isn't something else."

Peter Shillingsburg

"Oh, blimey," Jeremy Bullmore once said about creativity. "Clients know they want it; agencies know they've got to deliver it; but nobody knows what it is."[11]

So before we go too much further, it might be useful to pause for a moment and define what we mean by 'creativity'. What exactly is 'creative' advertising and how does it differ from the uncreative?

"Creativity is extremely difficult to define," says David Lubars, "but incredibly easy to identify."

David is Chief Creative Officer of BBDO, the most creatively awarded advertising network in the world for the past several years.[12] Which gives us some idea of how far up the food chain creativity's famed indefinability persists.

Bill Bernbach was quick to warn against worrying too much about it. "It's like love," he said of creativity. "The more you analyse it, the faster it disappears."

Even so, it'd be somewhat uncooperative to present the case for creativity while refusing to explain what we mean by 'creative' advertising. And, as David suggests, though we mightn't define creativity, there are a handful of things that, in the eyes of the most creative advertising and marketing people, easily identify the truly creative campaigns in advertising's pack.

American English Professor Peter Shillingsburg once said that "creativity is whatever isn't something else", echoing the commonly-held belief that creativity is most easily identified when something new is brought into existence out of nothing. Originality is the first and perhaps most unambiguous characteristic of creativity. Well-trodden territory is easily identified, and recycled ideas are unceremoniously disregarded by creative award judges.

"Great work should make you feel uncomfortable because it hasn't been done before," says Tony Davidson, Executive Creative Director of Wieden+Kennedy London. His agency, one of the most respected in the world for its creativity, is famous for legendary campaigns such as Nike's 'Run London' and Honda's 'Power of Dreams'. Speaking of the less creative ideas that occasionally slip through the W+K net, Tony says, "Ken Kier, head of Honda Europe, still to this day looks us in the eye and says 'it's not making me feel uncomfortable'. More brave clients like him please."

"To me, more creative marketing takes a really big step," says Jim McDowell, CEO of Mini, and Chief Marketing Officer of BMW during the period of their winning Cannes Advertiser of the Year. "It's not a small incremental add-on to something you've seen before. It takes a really big step in a direction that

Identifying creativity

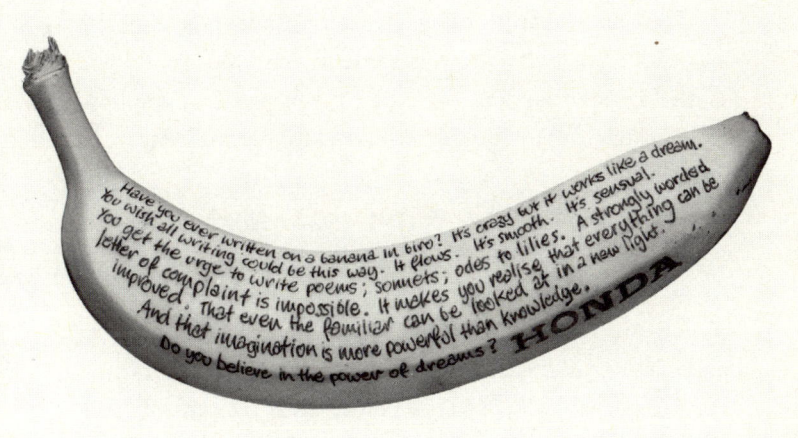

A popular execution from Honda's 'Power of Dreams' campaign by
Wieden+Kennedy London

I'd never even imagined. From that perspective you go 'oh wow, that truly is amazing and I wish I'd have thought of that myself'. That's the way it works in my mind."

The second characteristic of creative campaigns is probably best described as 'engagement'. The ability of an idea not only to communicate clearly, but also to be so interesting or enjoyable to engage with that people freely choose to spend time with it.

"The area which probably comes to mind when someone talks about 'creativity'," say researchers from Millward Brown, "is the big executional creative idea; the powerful or emotionally appealing creative hook, introduced to communicate more effectively."[13]

Uncreative work tends to start with a conviction that we simply need to clearly and comprehensively deliver marketing information, and that if we can do that in a way that's enjoyable to the consumer then that's 'nice to have', but not fundamentally necessary. That conviction stems from a belief that people naturally pay attention to, and consume, *all* the advertising that is put in front of them. That media in itself creates a willing audience for the message.

Conversely, the most creative work starts with the contrary belief that people naturally block advertising out and only consume the small amount of advertising that captures their interest. Media in itself makes an audience a possibility, but not a certainty - a thousand people passing by a billboard is not an audience of a thousand people. The true audience number is the number of people that actually notice and engage with the billboard, and that the quality of the idea determines the size of that audience.

The most creative work comes from a conviction that first we need to surprise and engage people, and to do so in a way that allows us to credibly and relevantly follow through with a marketing message.

"I think that first it has to touch something in me that makes me care," says Jim Stengel, former P&G Global Marketing Officer. "After we went to Cannes for the first time back in 2003, we decided that we were going to start measuring whether consumers told us 'I want to see that again'. And I think if people say that it touches them and makes them care, and they want to see it again, I think those are two very powerful ideas."

Saatchi & Saatchi's UK Director of Strategy Richard Huntington refers to this care factor as 'interestingness'. "Strategists spend vast swathes of time desperately trying to be right," he says, "with the result that the majority of strategic thinking is clichéd, lame and dreary."

His advice is to start by worrying about being *interesting*. "I guess my professional mantra of late has been summed up in the phrase 'it is vital to be interesting, it is merely important to be right'."[14]

"Then there is the execution," says Nick Worthington, our Executive Creative Director at Colenso. "What all great campaigns have in common is a great idea and great execution. If the head is seduced by 'the idea' then the heart is almost certainly won over by the execution."

Great 'craft' is the third characteristic of creatively superior work. Creative people tend to support the belief that any idea, no matter how good, has the potential to be anything from dismal failure to runaway success, and that the defining factor is its execution – those things like choice of music, typography or quality of photography.

"Ideas are just a multiplier of execution," agrees entrepreneur Derek Sivers. "To me, ideas are worth nothing unless executed. They are just a multiplier. Execution is worth millions."

Derek, the seminal online retailer tech millionaire who founded CD Baby, uses a chart to explain:

AWFUL IDEA = -1	NO EXECUTION = $1
WEAK IDEA = 1	WEAK EXECUTION = $1,000
SO-SO IDEA = 5	SO-SO EXECUTION = $10,000
GOOD IDEA = 10	GOOD EXECUTION = $100,000
GREAT IDEA = 15	GREAT EXECUTION = $1,000,000
BRILLIANT IDEA = 20	BRILLIANT EXECUTION = $10,000,000

"You need to multiply the two," he says. "The most brilliant idea, with no execution, is worth $20. The most brilliant idea takes great execution to be worth $20,000,000." [15]

Though we talk a lot about *ideas* in advertising, in fact what contributes to the creative quality, and ultimately the effectiveness of advertising, is as much to do with its execution. As BBH's John Hegarty is credited with saying, "a great ad is 80% idea and 80% execution". [16]

"At Leo Burnett we developed a 10-point scale to look at work in a conceptual way," says Michael Conrad, formerly Leo Burnett's Chief Creative Officer and now President of the Berlin School of Creative Leadership. "Called '7plus', it eliminated vague judgement and argumentation. We used 7plus to evaluate progress every three months by running a meeting looking at 1,000 to 1,200 pieces of work from all over the network. It did not take long until this practice moved from 'post' to 'pre'. You could call it 'Total Quality Management' in the ideas business. Within the first five years of 7plus, 27 Leo Burnett agencies were named Agency of the Year in their countries at least once."

The 7plus scale was made up of 10 categories, divided into three sections:

10   Most Inspiring in the World
9   New Standard in Communication
8   New Standard in Category

7   Excellence in Craft
6   Fresh Idea(s)
5   Innovative Strategy

4   Cliché
3   Non Competitive
2   Destructive
1   Appalling

"1 to 4 is what we wanted to avoid," says Michael. "8 to 10 is where we wanted to be. And 5 to 7 are qualities you need to have in order to avoid inferior work or to lay the tracks to superior work."

As well as helping identify the most creative work, the 7plus scale suggests something of a definition of uncreative work. In between the creative campaigns and those advertisements so poor as to be labelled 'appalling' or 'destructive' are campaigns that Michael and his team labelled 'non-competitive' and 'cliché'.

Saying the same thing as the other guy, or saying something that the consumer has heard time and time again, is the first sure sign of uncreativity. Fortunately, as tempting as it can sometimes be to make worn-out, non-competitive claims such as having the tastiest taste or producing the whitest whites, the idea of differentiation has largely been ingrained into the canon of accepted marketing wisdom.

However, encouragement to use clichéd executional ideas is more pervasive. In the mid-2000s, after being slapped on the hand for their highly original (and sometimes regulation-defying) advertising, New Zealand vodka brand 42 Below produced the following radio announcement:[17]

"Due to the regulations surrounding New Zealand alcohol advertising, all our future ads will be about three 'mates' in their mid to late twenties on a quest to find 'a good time'. This quest will involve them in various 'shenanigans' until they finally find satisfaction by discovering 42 Below Vodka at some unexpected tavern. These 'mates' must be average white males, one of whom must seem a bit 'goofy'. 42 Below will investigate the possibility of a token Maori mate appearing from time to time. New Zealand alcohol advertising regulations also stress that the three 'mates' will at some stage associate with three white females in denim shorts or bikinis, to show that they are not poofs. However, these women should not in any way distract them from completing their initial quest, which is to find 42 Below Vodka. The advert will contain three gags, and I say 'gags', every fifteen seconds, contemporary rock music and at least one scene in an old Holden, cleverly written so it doesn't imply drink driving of any sort. We trust you'll find these new 42 Below Vodka ads frickin' hilarious."

Although we make fun of the clichés, how often do we still seek refuge in the ultra-familiar? It's comforting to believe that formulaic advertising scenarios, albeit unexciting, won't risk being misunderstood or alienating groups of consumers. And yet how often do we need to see people offended by the clichés? "Do those companies think we're idiots or what?"

Four decades earlier, Leo Burnett himself had attempted a definition of creativity. It is, he said, "the art of establishing new and meaningful relationships between previously unrelated things in a manner that is relevant, believable, and in good taste, but which somehow presents the product in a fresh new light".

His words reflect a caution that creative leaders are often quick to impress on us. That, unlike the fields of art and entertainment, advertising isn't *just* about producing original, engaging and well-crafted ideas; and that the real trick of advertising is doing so in a way that solves the problem of selling a client's product.

James McGrath is Creative Chairman of Australia's Clemenger BBDO advertising network, his country's most awarded group of agencies in terms of both creativity and effectiveness. James' criteria for judging creative awards go beyond the artistic merits of the work.

"What great award-worthy and effective campaigns have that others don't would have to be their ability to make an extraordinary idea work only because of the vital inclusion of the product. In judging terms it's the foundation on which you begin to then take all the subsequent conceptual, intellectual and executional elements into account. From there it's a matter of relevance. Sure, an idea might be doing it like it's never been done before, but if it's a simple, vain and self-conscious affectation disconnected from the product, an insight, or most importantly the consumer, then it's nothing more than a self-serving exercise."

"My favourite creative work," agrees Tony Davidson, "makes me wonder 'how did they come up with that', and yet at the same time feel it is really right for that brand. That is a real skill. I guess in my work, I've always asked the question, 'why is that right for this brand?' You often see award-winning work which is just a sponsored joke that does little for the brand. Most of the best work I have been involved in has a deep insight or truth that has been uncovered by digging deep into the company or product. Advertising making stuff up feels wrong. That's why I am still really proud of work like 'Run London' that we launched 10 years ago and was a 360° integrated experience that tied back into product. And all of the great Honda work we have done comes from true insights."

In the 1990s, Donald Gunn produced his landmark study 'Do Award Winning Commercials Sell?' in which he showed that over 80% of awarded advertising had met or exceeded its client's objectives. We'll cover the study in detail later, but among Donald's conclusions is the advice that for creativity to be effective, it needs to be an amplifier of sound strategic thinking, rather than a replacement for it.

"The evidence is overwhelming," he says, "that well-focused commercials which are based on the right message and, *in addition*, deliver it and translate it freshly, charmingly, engagingly and intelligently work better than commercials with the right message but which lack these creative qualities."

As Hemingway advised, "the most essential gift for a good writer is a built-in, shockproof shit detector". The very best creative people seem to know not only how to *be* creative – how to find an innovative point of view, wrap it up in a fresh and engaging executional idea and then execute it with a high degree of craft quality – but importantly how to *use* creativity to solve problems and sell products. To create things of real value, rather than shit.

And so, in the interests of not analysing it until it disappears, that's probably what we mean by 'creativity'.

4. The case for originality

"In order to be irreplaceable one must always be different."

Coco Chanel

In 2005 in Auckland a group called Godmarks launched a campaign of billboards designed to generate a more positive feeling toward Christianity. White words on a black background from He Himself, they said things like, "I was just thinking about you", "I love everyone, even Christians", and my own favourite, "Well, you did ask for a sign".

At an end-of-year gathering, filled with the spirit of Christmas, I dared to speak some kind words about the campaign among a group of creative people.

The group hastened to recalibrate my view, pointing out that the campaign was a copy of an earlier American campaign, and in light of this poverty of originality, was utterly meritless.

An idealistic judgement, one might say. Regardless of whether or not the campaign was effective, it was no good because it wasn't 'original'. The evening wasn't spoiled with an argument, but the question had been asked: why do we have such an obsession with originality?

THE CASE FOR CREATIVITY

We all know it's true. An unoriginal idea, no matter how engaging or strategically sound, will struggle to make it out of most creative departments. The words 'it's been done' will fell the biggest of ideas in the coldest of blood.

The Godmarks campaign had proven effective in the USA, and was employed in New Zealand because of its prior performance. Yet the belief persisted that it would have been more virtuous to have created a purely original campaign, never mind that it might not have served Godmarks so well.

That conviction is both staunch and widespread. But the reasons for it are less apparent. Why do we advertising people have such an inhospitable response to the unoriginal?

Four years later, halfway through a pre-production meeting to finalise details of the filming of a new campaign for our local Vodafone client, our account director passed around an iPhone on which to watch a YouTube clip he'd been sent.

We were well past the point of no return on what we were sure was an original idea – staging a performance of Tchaikovsky's 1812 Overture using the TXT alert sounds of a thousand mobile phones.[18] So our discovery of an eerily similar film showing a performance of jingle bells using the 'ding' sounds of forty-nine microwaves was disconcerting.[19] We were innocent of any imitation, but we weren't certain others would see it that way.

THE CASE FOR CREATIVITY

Vodafone Symphonia (top); AKQA's Christmas video

It's only human to feel a sense of injustice when we learn of those who've knowingly passed off others' work as their own. Blogs at home and abroad are rife with accusatory posts spotlighting copycat advertising. Some of them are no doubt accurate – but being falsely accused is one of creativity's most common professional hazards.

There's almost as much damage in being *accused* of plagiarism as there is in plagiarism itself. Innocence is difficult to prove. "What are the chances!" you joke. And that's precisely what everybody else is thinking. What *are* the chances?

Two people conjuring up the same idea at the same time is regarded as highly suspicious. It seems a thoroughly improbable occurrence. It may be conceivable that two different people could have similar ideas, but at the same time?

And yet, surprisingly, it turns out to be entirely common.

In his New Yorker essay 'In The Air: Who Says Big Ideas Are Rare?', Malcolm Gladwell touches on the work of William Ogburn and Dorothy Thomas, who in 1922 created a surprisingly long list of major ideas that had been simultaneously had by different scientists and inventors.[20]

Frenchmen Charles Cros and Louis Ducos du Hauron both invented colour photography at the same time in the mid-nineteenth century. In 1608, the telescope was independently invented by Hans Lippershey, Zacharias Janssen and Jacob Metius. The thermometer is claimed by at least six different men. And historians estimate the typewriter was created in the eighteenth century, by separate inventors, 52 times across Europe and America.

These occurrences of multiple discovery turned out to be anything but rare. Ogburn and Thomas found 148 major examples of such multiplicity.

Evolution, so commonly attributed to Charles Darwin, was also discovered by Alfred Russel Wallace. Calculus was invented by both Isaac Newton and Gottfried Wilhelm Leibniz. The telegraph was pioneered simultaneously in 1837 by the Englishman Charles Wheatstone and the American Samuel Morse. And both the steamboat and the jet engine were designed by several independent engineers in the eighteenth and twentieth centuries, respectively.

In the 1960s, American sociologist Robert Merton furthered the study of multiplicity, concluding that "the pages of the history of science record thousands of instances of similar discoveries having been made by scientists working independently of one another. Sometimes the discoveries are simultaneous or almost so; sometimes a scientist will make a new discovery which, unknown to him, somebody else had made years before."

The title of Gladwell's essay spoke to the theory that ideas, rather than being born in the minds of their creators, are in fact 'in the air', to be discovered by anybody searching in the right direction at that particular moment. The sentiment reflects the words of Hungarian mathematician Farkas Bolyai, who in the nineteenth century suggested that "when the time is ripe for certain things, these things appear in different places in the manner of violets coming to light in early spring."

In 2003, Dan Futterman finished his screenplay 'Capote' within weeks of fellow biographer Douglas McGrath submitting 'Infamous'. The writers, completely unknown to each other, had chosen not only the same subject, but exactly the same period of Truman Capote's life. The history of filmmaking records dozens of such examples. 1998's 'The Truman Show' and 'EdTV' share an identical premise, as do 'Deep Impact' and 'Armageddon' from the same year. 'Groundhog Day' had a twin in '12:01', a TV movie of the same year. 'Lambada' was released on the same day in 1990 as 'The Forbidden Dance', also about the Lambada dance craze. 'Turner & Hooch' and 'K9', both about a police officer getting a dog for a partner, were released simultaneously in 1989. The novel 'Les Liaisons Dangereuses' was adapted as 'Dangerous Liasons' in 1988 and 'Valmont' in 1989. More recently, 'Coco avant Chanel' and 'Coco Chanel & Igor Stravinsky' were independently released within weeks of each other.

American writer Charles Fort also appeared to believe that ideas were 'in the air'. Trying to explain the six or seven inventions of the steam engine within a three-month window, he said, "I guess it was just steam engine time." That designation – 'steam engine time' – has since been used by some to describe those cases of a single idea appearing at once in several

David (left); Hermes

unconnected minds.

How fascinating a notion, that external conditions at specific times create an environment in which certain ideas become 'likely'.

And yet the theory offered scant solace for those of us working on the Vodafone campaign. Our fears of being gleefully exposed and unsympathetically trialled were not without good cause.

Copying somebody else's idea is creativity's most detestable of sins. It's cheating. It's scandalous. And in our highly competitive field, it's just the thing our contemporaries hope we've been up to.

So much so that perhaps originality has become a self-preservation mechanism. Maybe our single-minded pursuit of originality is simply the surest way to keep our reputation untainted.

Or could it be because originality of thought is a romantic trait, a mark displayed by artists and scientists of the sort of genius we covet for ourselves?

Advertising has occasional parallels with the art world, and most modern artists are as obsessed with originality as we are.

But this has not always been the case. Our modern notion that the artist's work must be original would have been completely foreign to the Egyptian, Chinese or Byzantine master.

Up until the end of the Renaissance, an artist who deliberately sought originality would have been considered mad rather than gifted. A great artist used to be a copyist – of the ancients, of nature, of the ideal form.

What Michelangelo did with 'David', the Greek sculptor Praxiteles had done eighteen centuries earlier with 'Hermes'. Vermeer's 'The Girl with the Pearl Earring' was often called 'The Mona Lisa of the North' for its similarities to Da Vinci's masterpiece. It wasn't a term of derision, rather a mark of respect for an artist who'd managed to replicate so successfully the effect of another master. Not until the eighteenth century were unpredictability and eccentricity seen as signs of genius.

The same goes for literature. Rather than writing original plays, Shakespeare appropriated sources and fashioned them anew, whereas modern writers are sensitive to any similarity of plot or prose. "Originality, not just innocence of plagiarism but the making of something really and truly new, set itself down as a cardinal literary virtue somewhere in the middle of the eighteenth century and has never since gotten up," says literary critic Thomas Mallon.

Today, originality is the yardstick against which most art is measured. American painter Robert Henri captured the artist's pursuit in 1923: "We are not here to do what has already been done."

In its December 31, 1999 issue, *Time* magazine revealed its list of the 100 most important people of the twentieth century.

At the top was Albert Einstein. The embodiment of scientific genius, Einstein's originality of thought is stupefying. Even those of genius themselves were perplexed by the notion of relativity. Nobel Prize-winning physicist Richard Feynman famously commented, "I still can't see how he thought of it."

Despite Einstein's genius, *Time's* choice to sit him atop its list was an interesting one. To people who think for a living, like other scientists, artists or even advertising creatives, Einstein is relevant. He was the ultimate thinker. He developed an understanding of relativity *just by thinking about it*. But to the rest of the world – the much larger group who don't spend their days in labs and studios – the great physicist's relevance is limited. One could argue that Martin Luther King's struggle for racial equality has had a greater impact on our everyday lives; that Churchill's tenacity in the face of fascism saved democracy; that Ford's vision of the motorcar changed everything; and that for their direct and tangible influence on all of our lives, one of them should take precedence over any theoretical scientist.

So why the kudos for Einstein, a man most famous for thinking up something that most of us don't even understand?

Perhaps the answer lies in the fact that the twentieth century was characterised by an obsession with original thinking. We evolved from a culture that rewarded conformity and tradition to one that celebrated individuality and innovation. This democracy of thought is what many would consider the greatest cultural shift of the twenty-first century.

Within this context, original thinking has become loved and revered – both as a symbol of freedom and an agent of progress. Those we believe to be geniuses we hold in the esteem that earlier generations reserved for royalty. Albert Einstein is King. Creative people can hardly be blamed for striving toward originality. Society worships it.

But what role does originality play in advertising effectiveness? It's all very well to value originality in and of itself, but as Mark Twain said, "the man with a new idea is a crank until the idea succeeds".

When Bill Bernbach observed that "you cannot sell a man who isn't listening", he was inferring that more original advertising was more likely to capture attention. That originality was the key to making your campaign one of the few that didn't go unnoticed. He was proven right when half a century later, five groups of university academics from the USA and Europe studied the effects of originality. They all found that the more original ads were more likely to stand out and be noticed.[21]

But does originality do more than merely make campaigns stand out? Does it, for example, enhance the *appeal* of creative work?

An analysis of successful creativity in the entertainment industry draws a frustrating conclusion: the more original the product, the less it seems to appeal to most people.

It's easy to cringe at the success of the Backstreet Boys. Poster boys for a generation of derivative, formulaic, highly engineered pop, they have sold a staggering 130 million albums globally, including 32 million copies of their eponymous 1995 debut.

Contrast them with one of their most lauded, influential and original peers: Radiohead. Considered by many critics to be the greatest album of all time, 'OK Computer' has appeared at or near the top of virtually every major 'best albums' list, from *Rolling Stone* to *The Guardian*. And yet this masterpiece has sold only four million copies worldwide. It's difficult to see the justice in the Backstreet Boys' debut album outselling one of the most original creative efforts of the twentieth century by a factor of eight.

Bjork, one of the most innovative and fearless songwriters of all time, has sold around ten million albums during her 20-year career. By comparison, Dido sold 13 million copies of her debut album 'No Angel' – which one critic described as "music to microwave lasagne to" – dwarfing Bjork's entire career in 52 minutes flat.

The box office paints us a similar picture. As at 2008, 40 films from history had grossed over $500 million globally.[22] Twenty-six were adaptations from popular books or comics (such as 'Lord of the Rings' and 'Spider-Man'), sequels to previously successful franchises ('Star Wars: Episode 1 - The Phantom Menace', 'The Matrix Reloaded') or adaptations

THE CASE FOR CREATIVITY

Backstreet Boys

of historical stories ('Titanic', 'The Passion of the Christ'), rendering them unoriginal from conception. The remaining 14 big hitters – such as 'Independence Day', 'Ghost' and 'Armageddon' – all follow the formulaic three-act linear structure that Hollywood demands.

When screenwriters pen a film that they hope will be made in Los Angeles, they're required to follow a prescriptive set of rules that determine the length and structure of the film. The fact is that Hollywood leaves very little room for originality because most people tend not to enjoy original films. Sure, films such as Cannes Palme d'Or winners 'Pulp Fiction' and 'Fahrenheit 911' and popular classics 'Forrest Gump' and 'ET' have met with both critical acclaim and enormous box office success. But the rule prevails – if we're looking to entertain a mass audience, we're better to show them something they're familiar with.

But what if, rather than to entertain, we want to *persuade* an audience? Is originality more helpful than familiarity when forming an argument?

At Ogilvy London in 2004, planner Olivia Johnson was conducting research for her client, Dove, with the aid of feminist icons like Susie Orbach and Gloria Steinem. The resulting report, 'The Real Truth About Beauty', showed that just 9% of women considered themselves 'attractive', 60% strongly agreed

Dove's 'Campaign for Real Beauty'

that 'society expects women to enhance their physical attractiveness' and 68% strongly agreed that 'the media and advertising set an unrealistic standard of beauty that most women can never achieve'.[23]

Olivia responded with a strategy to question the image of beauty as defined and pumped out by the beauty industry. And so the Dove 'Campaign for Real Beauty' was born.[i]

Well, almost.

The senior managers at Dove were predominantly male. They'd built a massive global business partly through advertising which, like all their cosmetic industry peers, used aspirational images of beautiful women. To suggest to them that they should shoulder the weight of an entire culture's manipulation and crusade philanthropically against it could easily have been dismissed as preposterous.

To give the strategy hope, Account Director Daryl Fielding suggested a highly original way to convince Dove of Olivia's thinking. They'd find the daughters of those mostly male senior managers. They'd film them talking candidly about how imperfect the images in the media made them feel. Then, at the creative presentation to Dove, they'd show those tapes to their fathers.

It was a powerful argument. Businessmen are used to

---

[i] *Over the years I've heard several people conjecture that Dove's Campaign for Real Beauty was ineffective from a product sales point of view. It's worth noting that the campaign won effectiveness awards in the UK, USA and Canada, and that all three effectiveness case studies (all of which are available in the public domain) were based on product sales growth rather than simply brand or communications measures.*

making rational, objective judgements, after taking in research presentations full of graphs and charts. An appeal from your own daughter is completely original. The campaign was approved and rolled out globally.

But would the outcome have been different if, in the weeks leading up to Olivia's presentation, other suppliers had pitched to those men, using video of their families to make the point?

Social psychologists in the late 1970s found that as people were repeatedly exposed to a 'persuasive message', they developed 'counterarguments', reducing their agreement with, and thus the persuasiveness of, the original argument.[24] That, over time, we develop a kind of 'immunity' to being 'sold to' with arguments we've seen or heard before.

Our psychological reaction to arguments is similar to our physical reaction to viruses. Our immune system, the first time it's exposed to a foreign body, has a tricky time beating it. However, when the virus returns, it's innocuous. We have no trouble dealing with an unoriginal virus. Likewise, an unoriginal argument is likely to suffer defeat at the hands of our cognitive immune system. There's an ability in all of us to think our way out of even the most robust argument given enough time.

A fresh argument, however, has the opportunity to make it through the mind's defences before they have time to beat it.

In 2008 marketing professors at Indiana University found this to hold true in practice. Testing advertising of varying levels of originality, they found that more original ads not only attracted more attention, but also reduced consumers' resistance to persuasion. "This is an important finding," they said, "because any strategy that can reduce resistance to persuasion and make consumers more open-minded can have a significant impact on brand purchase intentions."[25]

The ability of original ideas to stand out and be remembered is difficult to refute, but further to merely getting noticed, an original argument has a better chance of persuading people because they haven't yet developed *cognitive immunity* to it.

The nineteenth-century historian Thomas Carlyle said "originality is a thing we constantly clamour for, and constantly quarrel with". He was speaking in and of the Victorian era, but the sentiment rings true today. We clamour for originality and it's rewarded handsomely on the stages of our award shows, but in boardrooms and strategy meetings we constantly quarrel with it. What makes an original piece of communication, for example, a better bet than replicating something that we can see has worked in the past? Are we sure we're not being creative just for the sake of it?

Well, originality has been proven to aid in cut-through and persuasion. It's been proven to make communication more effective. But it also moves us forward. Keeping the muscle of originality well toned means we continually find new ways to engage with consumers, new ways to keep advertising palatable to society and new ways to differentiate products and brands.

As another of *Time's* 100 most important people, Coco Chanel, said: "In order to be irreplaceable one must always be different."

I'm with her.

5. The case for creative advertising
(according to Donald Gunn, the IPA
and McKinsey & Company)

"The extent to which they turned out to be more effective than non-creatively-awarded campaigns still remains astonishing to me."

Peter Field

"In our business there is a substantial body of opinion that is dismissive if not scornful about creative awards. These industry colleagues – and they exist both at clients and in agencies – take the view that awards are basically a frivolity, and are wholly irrelevant, indeed probably counterproductive, to the main business in hand – the selling of products and services."[26]

These, in 1996, were the words of a troubled Donald Gunn, then working at one of the world's most creatively-awarded agencies.

"They assume and believe and also will broadcast the view that winning awards and selling products are, for the most part, and in some fundamental way, mutually exclusive. They clearly suspect that the motives that go into an ad that wins awards and an ad that is designed to sell are different. This makes a mockery of the value creative people place upon awards, which to them represent the highest recognition by their peers."

This rift eventually unsettled Donald to the point of action. "At Leo Burnett," he remembers, "I was the impetuous volunteer who conceived of, then carried out, the 'Do Award-Winning Commercials Sell?' study. This consisted of identifying the 400 most awarded commercials and campaigns in the world from 1992-1995, then painstakingly gathering in the 400 case histories."

The basic objective of his study was simple: to find out, once and for all, whether that commonly held cynicism about creative awards was right or wrong.

To analyse such a large pool of campaigns, Donald and his team reviewed the work of 129 agencies in 26 countries, arriving at a set of campaigns that had between them won 1,483 major creative awards.

Causing what must have been a record quarter in agency telecommunications costs, they called the CEO or Executive Creative Director of all 129 agencies, introduced the study and followed up with a simple questionnaire requesting the objectives and results of each campaign. If it had met or exceeded objectives, they required quantified evidence. If it hadn't, they asked why not.

"The result was pretty compelling," Donald recalls. "86.5% of them had been associated with marketplace success." Three hundred and thirty-six of those 400 campaigns had met or exceeded the objectives set by their clients.

Of course, that left 54 underachievers. "A number of the cases failed to achieve objectives and to move business ahead. There were also four cases in the category 'Client considers successful, but no quantified data are available'. We counted these as No's."

The remaining huge majority were examples of effective advertising. Some of them modestly so, but "at the top end of the study was a group of cases – more than 100 of them, over 25% of the total – where the level of business success was not just good, not just very good, but could more appropriately be described as amazing. Way beyond any increase you'd see written down in even the most aggressive marketing plan."

An emphatic result, but how accurate was this data? Would agencies have told Donald and his team if the advertising hadn't worked?

"Firstly," says Donald, "I was dealing on a confidential basis with very senior people at the world's best advertising agencies. 54 of whom, by the way, did tell me that the advertising hadn't worked. My own belief is that good advertising people at this level are more interested in getting at the truth than in being proved personally right. Secondly, for 56 of the cases {the candidates for use as examples in the resulting presentation at the 1996 Cannes Advertising Festival}, I went back to the agencies for clearance to use the results and detailed numbers they'd provided. So they now knew that their data were liable to be quoted before 2,000 or so delegates at Cannes, including people from their own market or with intimate knowledge of their category. There was not a single case in the 56 where anyone back-tracked on their claims or wanted to downsize any numbers."

Donald and his colleagues at Leo Burnett felt the result was conclusive. "Which basically may suggest," they said, "that award show judges and our clients' customers have a whole lot in common in the way they react to advertising."

"But 1996," Donald admitted in 2010, "is a long time ago."

Three years after the conclusion of his landmark study, Donald ended three decades at Leo Burnett to launch his inaugural Gunn Report. The report is based, he says, "on a very simple idea. It combines the winners lists from all the major advertising award contests in the world to establish the annual worldwide league tables for the advertising industry.

"Totting up award shows for a living might seem like a somewhat frivolous endeavour," he admitted at a recent UK conference, "but it has a serious underpinning. For I devoutly believe in the power of creativity to produce sales for the immediate present at the same time as it builds reputation for the long haul."

The Gunn Report's raison d'etre is to rank agencies and campaigns according to their creativity. It has nothing to do with effectiveness. But, inadvertently, it had grown into a set of data that would prove invaluable in the *study* of effectiveness.

"It's something I'd been thinking about for years," says UK marketing consultant Peter Field. "A few years ago I heard Donald Gunn give his presentation on creativity. It occurred to me that he had this fantastic database of creativity, and I had my hands on a rather handy database of effectiveness."

Peter, an independent contractor to the UK's Institute of Practitioners in Advertising, was for the second time mining the IPA Effectiveness Databank case studies to help the IPA and their member advertising agencies understand what led to more effective advertising.

"Donald spoke very academically about creativity and that's a rare commodity – somebody who obviously has his finger very firmly on the creative pulse, but can also put a presentation together and do a bit of number crunching. It took me about three years to get it off the ground, but when I put the proposal to Donald he leapt at it."

His proposal to Donald was to fuse the Gunn Report database of creatively-awarded campaigns with the IPA Effectiveness Databank to examine the link between creativity and effectiveness.

"Increasingly I think the climate is more towards understanding the benefits of creative awards," observes Peter. "P&G have had a famous conversion on this – from ten or fifteen years ago forbidding any of their agencies from even entering creative awards to now pitching up at Cannes every year feeling that they can learn from that. So there've been some very conspicuous client conversions to the cause over that period of time."

The IPA's Director of Marketing Janet Hull agrees. "There have been signs that attitudes have begun to move in favour of creative awards in recent years," she says. But the scepticism that had so troubled Donald Gunn in the nineties still exists. "By no means all advertisers believe that creative awards hold any commercial value. Creative awards are still often seen as a distraction from the business of selling."

"And it's difficult to pin down the reasons why," continues Peter. "I think it's a number of things. It's partly the excesses of the past. Clearly the clients who were around in the eighties and nineties probably did see a less business-like approach to creativity in agencies.

"I think another reason is the kind of stuff that gets taught in marketing, even today. Anyone who's gone into marketing has come out of it with classical marketing training, the kind of stuff that gets taught in colleges. It's so well off the pace, it's so out of touch with modern thinking and understanding of how the brain works. And if you've come from that kind of educational background you could be forgiven for thinking that how to sell a product is, you know, functional benefits, communication of messages; it's about hard selling. And all that creativity bit is loose-cannon thinking that occasionally works out but, by and large, is pretty dangerous stuff.

"And then of course there's the cosh that's on marketing these days. Marketing used to be a much more trusted discipline within companies. But if you talk to most CEOs these days they regard marketing as a pretty flaky discipline. It's not commercially focused and can't really be trusted. That's true of Chief Executives and certainly true of Finance Directors who see marketing as flaky and loose. And if they think marketing is flaky you can bet your bottom dollar they think ad agencies are flaky squared. You know, off in la la land."

Peter's 2010 study, 'The Link Between Creativity and Effectiveness',[27] sought to answer the same question that Donald had asked 14 years earlier. Only, to put a more sturdy case to the CEOs and Finance Directors, he'd ask the question with significantly more data, more independence[ii] and more rigour.

[ii] *How independent is Peter Field? "First of all," he says, "I don't work for the IPA. I'm an independent consultant – a subcontractor to them on a number of projects that involve data analysis. They use me when they want an independent analytical approach. I'm also not part of the agency world. I haven't been for the last 13 years. I do very little work directly with agencies. Almost all of my work is on the client side. So I've no axe to grind about this. I'm not interested particularly in proving this link for the sake of it. And I certainly don't get any remuneration as a result of these findings. I just saw this as an interesting piece of analysis in the databank that I wanted to further. And the results are as they are, the data's there. Anyone can inspect that data, it's robust and in the public domain."*

"When I first spoke to Donald I said, 'I can't guarantee you're going to get positive findings, but the omens are pretty good'."

Three years earlier, along with DDB's Les Binet, Peter had published 'Marketing in the Era of Accountability', another combing of the IPA's databank for effectiveness clues.

"In it there's a whole section on communication strategy," says Peter, "and what we found was that emotional campaigns are much more effective. And in particular, those campaigns that get talked about a lot – the ones we call 'fame' campaigns – they're the most effective of all. They're conspicuously the most effective campaigns out there.

"I was fairly certain that creative judges would be heavily skewed toward, firstly, emotional campaigns, and secondly, ones that had this kind of talkability about them. I imagined that would be very much the kind of thing that creative judges would be looking for. So I felt there was a pretty good chance that creatively-awarded campaigns would be fishing in a pool of rich effectiveness because the creative judges would be looking for the right sort of things.

"That was the hypothesis, and that's how it turned out – that's exactly what they seem to be looking for. If you look at creatively-awarded campaigns they're much more likely to be emotional, and very much more likely to have generated these strong word-of-mouth effects and both of those things correlate with effectiveness.

"But even so, the extent to which they turned out to be more effective than non-creatively-awarded campaigns still remains astonishing to me – I still find it difficult to quite believe the extent of that difference."

'The Link Between Creativity and Effectiveness' begins with 257 IPA case studies. Those represent every campaign to have been recognised as effective at the IPA's Effectiveness Awards (globally considered the toughest and most credible advertising effectiveness awards programme) since 2000. Why 2000? This was the inaugural year of the Gunn Report, and so these 257 campaigns are those capable of being analysed according to *both* creative award and effectiveness performance.

Of these campaigns, 46 were creatively-awarded, and 211 were not, establishing the two groups to compare and contrast.

At first glance, this seems to suggest that effective campaigns are predominantly *uncreative*, making more of a case for *uncreativity*. However, a deeper analysis reveals the opposite.

"If you take the total number of ads made each year, about one in 7000 pick up a creative award," says Peter, illustrating how rare creatively-awarded work is, and therefore how statistically unlikely it is to show up at effectiveness award shows.

About a hundredth of a percent of advertising in general is creatively-awarded. But among highly effective campaigns, i.e. campaigns effective enough to win an IPA Effectiveness Award,

18% are creatively-awarded. That's an over-index of 128,500 for the statisticians out there, suggesting that creatively-awarded campaigns are orders of magnitude more likely to be effective.

"But this is not certain proof," the study hastens to remind us, "and so we shall examine whether the 18% of creatively-awarded campaigns outperformed the 82% of non-awarded campaigns in hard business terms."

Had the creatively-awarded group differed from the non-awarded group in any meaningful way it would have skewed the result. For example, say the creatively-awarded campaigns were all from growing categories, but the non-awarded ones were in stagnant categories, then the awarded campaigns would have had a head start. Peter was careful to contrast the two groups on measures of market share, category life stage, leader vs challenger, launches and re-launches, use of communication channel, and industry sector. He found that the two groups were evenly matched across all measures. Safe in the knowledge that the fight was fair, Peter put the two cohorts into the ring.

His first enquiry was into the efficiency of each group. Back in 'Marketing in the Era of Accountability', he and Les Binet had coined the term 'excess share of voice' (ESOV), which describes the situation of a brand's share of advertising spend in its category being greater than its market share. The effect of ESOV was invariably that the brand's market share grew.

On average, if you bought ten points of ESOV, you'd get 1.1% market share growth.

Very efficient campaigns would achieve more than 1.1% share growth for ten points of ESOV, and less efficient ones would achieve less than 1.1%.

So first he calculated the ESOV effects of the non-awarded campaigns. They worked out at 0.5% market share growth per ten points of ESOV. Well under the average.

Next he measured the creatively-awarded campaigns. On average, they generated 5.7% market share growth per ten points of ESOV. *Over 11 times greater than the non-awarded average.*

What this means is that the return on media investment for a highly creative campaign is on average 11 times higher. Or looking at it another way, to get the same result, you need to spend 11 times more media money on an uncreative production than you do on a highly creative one.

The intriguing second finding was that the creatively-awarded campaigns were much more *certain* to achieve that effectiveness result.

In the case of the non-awarded campaigns, the average was 0.5% market share growth per ten points of ESOV. But this average was frequently deviated from, revealing a degree of confidence of 87%.

THE CASE FOR CREATIVITY

The 1.1:1 Efficiency Advantage of Creatively-Awarded Campaigns over Non-Creatively Awarded Campaigns

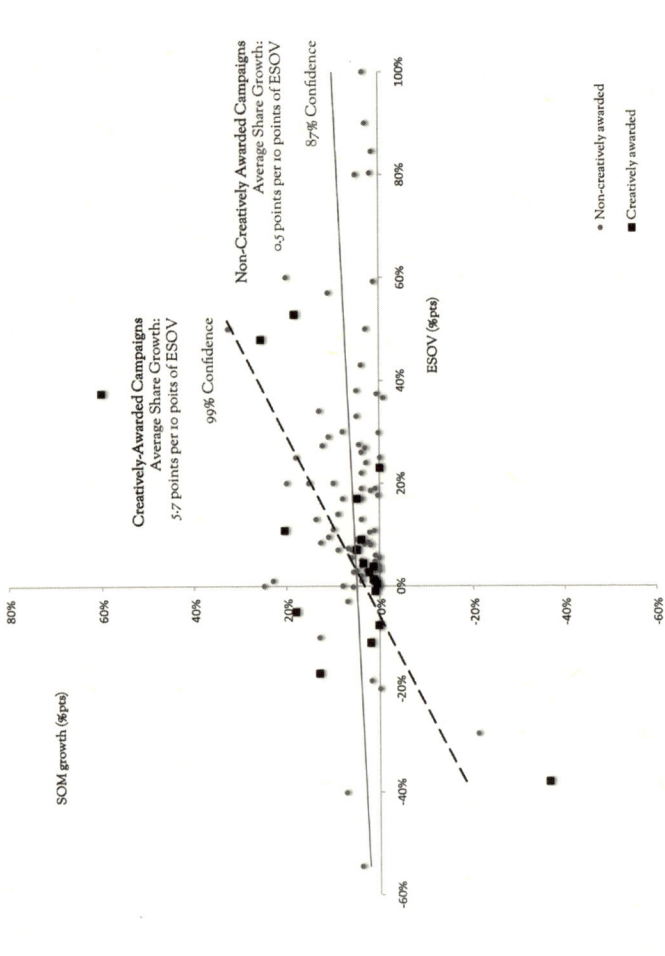

In the case of the creatively-awarded campaigns, that degree of confidence was 99.9%.

What this implies is that less creative campaigns are not only less efficient, but also less predictable than creatively-awarded ones – something of a departure from the perceived notion that a more creative approach is a less certain one.

"The paradoxical finding is that the correlation between creativity and efficiency of spend is stronger with creatively-awarded campaigns than with non-creatively-awarded ones," says Peter. "So the suggestion is in fact that creatively-awarded campaigns are more reliably effective than non-creatively-awarded ones. That flies in the face of accepted wisdom that creativity is a bit hit-and-miss. Clients in general management roles often have a preference for things that are less efficient but more certain rather than more efficient and less certain. There's that perception that creativity is very hit-and-miss. Although this paradoxical finding suggests that maybe that isn't true."

Our managing director at Colenso has a habit of dividing marketers into two groups – those he says are 'in it to win' and those who are 'in it not to lose'. What he means is that some clients will go for higher risk and higher reward in order to win big, and others will go for lower risk and lower reward in order to minimise their risk of losing.

What Peter's work suggests is that whether you're in it to win, or in it not to lose, you're much better off with a more

THE CASE FOR CREATIVITY

Creatively-Awarded Campaigns More Effective at Generating Large Business Effects at Both Low and High Spends

creative approach. Creatively-awarded campaigns are shown to be both lower risk *and* higher reward.

Peter's next question was whether, beyond media spend efficiency, the creatively-awarded campaigns were better at generating what he calls 'large business effects'. Those are top box scores for serious sales metrics such as penetration, share growth or profit growth (the kinds of results the finance director cares about, as opposed to softer communication tracking or brand health measures).

The analysis showed that at high levels of spend, the creatively-awarded campaigns were 10% more likely to generate those 'large business effects' than the non-awarded ones.

More interestingly, at lower levels of spend the creatively-awarded campaigns performed even better. At 27% more likely to generate 'large business effects', the creatively-awarded campaigns again showed much higher return on investment.

Then Peter asked perhaps the most fascinating question of his study. He asked whether those campaigns that are the *most* creatively-awarded are also the *most* effective.

Again it was Donald Gunn's work that enabled such a question to be asked. Each awarded campaign has a Gunn Report score, which increases according to the quantity and quality of creative awards won.

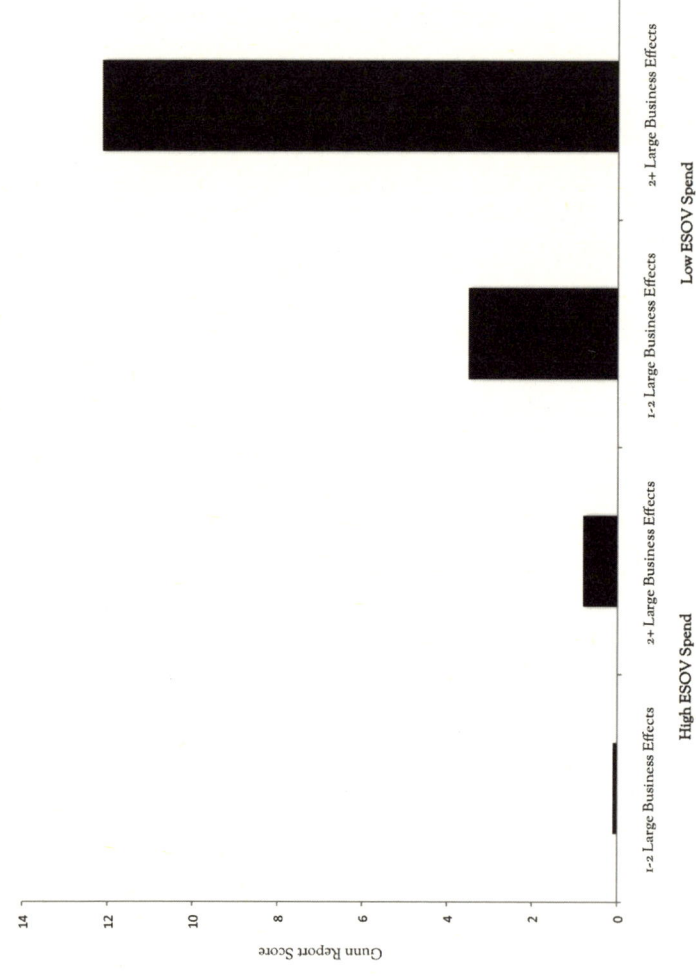

The Most Creatively-Awarded Campaigns are Also the Most Effective

"To pick up a point in the Gunn Report," says Peter, "you have to have won a fairly important creative award. Not always quite as posh as Cannes, but these are the major creative awards. They refuse to reveal exactly which award schemes they count, because they don't want to be seen to prejudice award schemes. But we know that the famous ones are in there, the ones that most creative people respect around the world."

Peter was able to look at the creatively-awarded campaigns that had been the most effective, and see whether they also had the highest Gunn Report scores.

"In theory," he observed, "if creativity is good for effectiveness then greater creativity ought to be better."

He divided the campaigns into two groups. The less effective first group included those campaigns that had achieved a low number (0-1) of very large business effects. The more effective second group included those that had achieved a high number (2+).

He then calculated the average Gunn Report score of each group.

The less effective group had an average Gunn Report score of 2.0 points.

The more effective group's score was 3.1, demonstrating, albeit crudely, that as advertising gets more creative, it also gets more effective.

To add further depth to this aspect of the study, Peter brought media spend into the equation. Would those campaigns that achieved a high number of very large business effects on a smaller spend turn out to be much more creative than those that achieved them on a large spend?

Again the findings were conclusive. The average Gunn Report score of the campaigns that achieved a high number of very large business effects on a large spend was 0.8 points, whereas the score for those that had achieved those very large business effects on a small spend – i.e. the campaigns that punched well above their media weights and delivered the greatest ROI – was 12.1 points. The most effective campaigns were also the most creative.

As the study concludes, "The greater the level of creativity, the greater the level of effectiveness."

Or, as McKinsey & Company put it, "the more creative a campaign, the higher the likelihood that the featured product will sell."[28]

In 2006 the Dusseldorf office of McKinsey had undertaken a study to quantify the success of German marketing campaigns. Some 100 television commercials submitted for the 2005 German effectiveness awards were examined, with changes in market share used as the measure of business impact.

They found that while the performance of less creative campaigns varied, the more creative campaigns were all high achievers in terms of business success.

McKinsey discovered what Donald Gunn had found a decade earlier and what Peter Field would find four years later: That more creative campaigns are more effective, and more reliably effective.

They generate more large business results than less creative campaigns. They're more efficient – they produce better results on much lower levels of media spend than less creative campaigns. And what's more, highly creative campaigns are more *certain* to produce those results than less creative campaigns.

The world's most prestigious management consulting firm[29] had clear advice for marketers. "Other things being equal," they said, "creativity is an advertiser's best bet."

THE CASE FOR CREATIVITY

6. How creativity makes advertising more effective
(according to Bill Bernbach & a tweed of academics*)

* 'tweed' is a collective noun for academics, proposed on all-sorts.org, an online collection of unofficial collective nouns.

THE CASE FOR CREATIVITY

"I warn you against believing that advertising is a science."

Bill Bernbach
Doyle, Dane & Bernbach

By the time DDB founder Bill Bernbach died in New York City in 1982, he'd made a case for creativity so strong it had completely redefined both the structure of advertising agencies and the nature of their product. During advertising's 'creative revolution', Bernbach put forward ideas about creativity that were expressed so persuasively and so memorably that they stuck just as fast as truths to the ideology of our industry.

But they weren't, in those days, known to be truths. Bernbach believed in creativity wholeheartedly, and expressed those beliefs with indomitable conviction. Albeit, they were only beliefs. Like everybody, Bernbach had been exposed only to his own tiny set of personal experience.

Until a full decade after he died, there was no evidence that his words were any more than just great ads for creativity. There'd been no academic interest in advertising creativity. Whether it worked or how it worked – these weren't questions

THE CASE FOR CREATIVITY

Bill Bernbach

being asked by researchers on anything other than a case-by-case basis in pre-testing or tracking research.

Half a century on, we know for sure that Bernbach was right. His words really were those of somebody with an innate understanding of human nature and its relationship with creativity.

Not only do we now know that creativity *does* work, we also have a fairly deep understanding of *how* it makes advertising more effective, thanks to the work of several teams of university academics from across the world.

"I warn you against believing that advertising is a science," Bernbach said. And the creation of it can never be, for so many conspicuous reasons. But perhaps he'd forgive us for borrowing from science to understand *why* he was right, and to revisit the unforgettable aphorisms he used to illuminate some of advertising's brightest years.

"If your advertising goes unnoticed, everything else is academic."

Bernbach's inference was that more creative advertising is more likely to stand out and be noticed.

In 2002 researchers at Tilburg University in The Netherlands sought to explore the relationship between originality in advertising and the attention paid to that advertising.[30]

Using eye tracking technology, they observed the attention levels of consumers as they read two magazines containing 58 print advertisements ranging from unoriginal to highly original. Using infrared corneal reflection eye tracking, the participants' eye movements were recorded as they read the magazines.

The originality of the ads was measured according to how surprising and unique the executions were, and how little they looked like other ads.

They found that increased levels of originality promoted increased and more intense attention to the advertisement and to the brand in those advertisements.

No fewer than four other groups of academics asked the same question about creativity and salience.[31] They all reached the same conclusion.

Creativity's first effect is that it makes advertising more likely to stand out and be noticed among the 3,000 or so commercial messages that consumers are besieged with daily.

"The difference between the forgettable and the enduring is artistry."

Bernbach believed that uncreative advertising would be forgotten, whereas more creative work would live on in the minds of consumers.

In 2005 research participants at the University of South

Carolina were shown a TV show with ten minutes of advertising content embedded in the breaks. The study contrasted 40 Communication Arts Award-winning commercials against a control group of 40 randomly selected 30-second spots from the same period that had not won any advertising creative awards.[32]

Unaided recall was tested immediately after the show, and then again one week later.

The result in both cases was that the creative commercials were significantly (two to nine times) more likely to be recalled unprompted than the control commercials.

Creativity's second effect is that it makes advertising more likely to be remembered, and more likely not to end up one of the 2,998 messages that go unrecalled each day.

"Word of mouth is the best medium of all."

Bernbach said this decades ago. Although it might seem like common knowledge today, he'd cottoned on to the power of conversation long before it became fashionable. As described in the previous chapter, highly creative campaigns are far more likely to drive word of mouth, and campaigns that drive word of mouth have been shown to be the most effective of all from a hard business results point of view. Creativity's third effect is driving the brand out of paid-for media and into the conversations of consumers.

> **"Getting a product known isn't the answer. Getting it WANTED is the answer. Some of the best known product names have failed."**

Bernbach knew that spending vast amounts on uncreative advertising would buy brand awareness, but that brand awareness isn't in itself persuasive. He believed that a more creative approach would help persuade consumers to buy a product.

Creativity's fourth and most powerful effect is in making advertising more persuasive.

Bernbach had ideas about why, exactly, people felt more persuaded by creative advertising. "You can say the right thing about a product and nobody will listen," he said. "You've got to say it in a way that people will feel in their gut. Because if they don't feel it, nothing will happen."

Bernbach believed in the ability of creativity to persuade on the basis that it made people more open to listening to and believing the rational information contained within. Through connecting with people in a less rational and more visceral way, creativity breaks down the barriers of mistrust and scepticism, leaving consumers more likely to believe what the brand has to say.

In 2009 Professors at the University of Wisconsin-Milwaukee and Indiana University created a pool of 50 creative award-winning ads and 50 'average' TV ads randomly recorded from major TV networks. Subjects were shown a selection of the ads within a section of 'Entertainment Tonight', then questioned on the persuasiveness of those ads.[33]

The findings were that the creatively-awarded ads triggered greater purchase intent, and that this was because they measurably increased open-mindedness and curiosity. Consumers let their defences down more for the creative advertising, allowing themselves to be sold to more readily. "This is an important finding," said the researchers, "because consumers are often sceptical and closed-minded when processing information from a vested-interest source, so they are unlikely to change existing beliefs and attitudes based on ad claims. Accordingly, any strategy that can reduce resistance to persuasion and make consumers more open-minded can have a significant impact on brand purchase intentions."

"Properly practised creativity can make one ad do the work of ten."

Bernbach was actually wrong on this one. Properly practised creativity can, as detailed in the previous chapter, make one ad do the work of *11*.

And it does so not with some one-dimensional impact, but with a four-stage combination of effects that work together to deliver a result far more efficiently than advertising ever can without the power of creativity.

First, more creative advertising stands out from the clutter, differentiating itself among a daily barrage of 3,000 commercial messages. Then, it makes you remember it. It sticks in your mind to guide you toward the brand it's advertising in the days following its viewing. Thirdly, you're much more likely to talk about it with others, and those conversations have been shown to have the greatest effect of all on sales. And lastly, creativity persuades you. It breaks down your barriers of scepticism and cuts through your cognitive immune system, making you far more likely to believe the advertiser and to act on that belief.

That, according to two decades of academic research, is how creativity makes advertising more effective.

7. The case for creative companies

THE CASE FOR CREATIVITY

"We'd been through the dark ages. And then we had the enlightenment."

Jim Stengel
Former Global Marketing Officer, P&G

At the 2009 Cannes International Festival of creativity, their Advertiser of the Year award was presented to Volkswagen.

Perennial darlings of the Côte d'Azur, Volkswagen's history tallies nearly 150 Cannes Lions including five Grands Prix and the award for the best commercial ever for Bill Bernbach's 1963 Beetle 'Snowplow' spot.

The Advertiser of the Year award recognised a particularly fertile 2008 for Volkswagen and their agencies DDB and Almap BBDO. No less than 15 separate campaigns for the brand were awarded at Cannes, D&AD and Clio. In terms of advertising creativity, it was an exceptional year, even for Volkswagen.

But that wasn't the only remarkable thing about Volkswagen's 2008. In a record year of trading for the Porsche-owned carmaker, Volkswagen's share price swelled 89% to close on an all-time New Year high of €283.[34]

The previous year, when many of those award-winning campaigns ran, the stock market performance was similarly impressive at 74% growth.

Across the 2000s, Volkswagen's average annual share price rise was an admirable 46%. But during the period of their most abundant creativity, the gain was almost double at 82%. During that same period the S&P500 fell nearly 16%,[35] illustrating how brightly Volkswagen outshone the market.

It would be far-fetched to claim that those award-winning campaigns drove the VOW.DE share price. But it's interesting to observe that Volkswagen's most prolific period of stock market success coincides precisely with their most prolific period in terms of creativity. We'd be forgiven for passing it off as a happy coincidence. But what's intriguing is how eerily often this coincidence seems to occur.

The previous year, Cannes' Advertiser of the Year was P&G. The story of marketing chief Jim Stengel's creative ambition for P&G is legendary, culminating in fourteen 2007 Cannes Lions for an organisation historically pilloried for its conservatism and unoriginality.

On December 12, 2007, P&G hit their all-time share price high of $74.67. Two months earlier, in an article titled 'P&G Share Price Soars', *Cosmetics International* magazine reported that "declining consumer spending, a jittery US housing market and rising interest rates might worry some companies, but

The case for creative companies

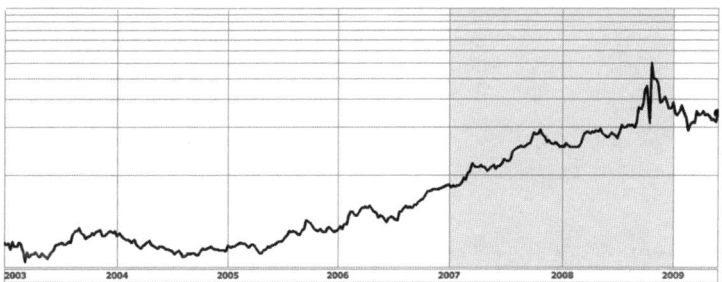

Volkswagen

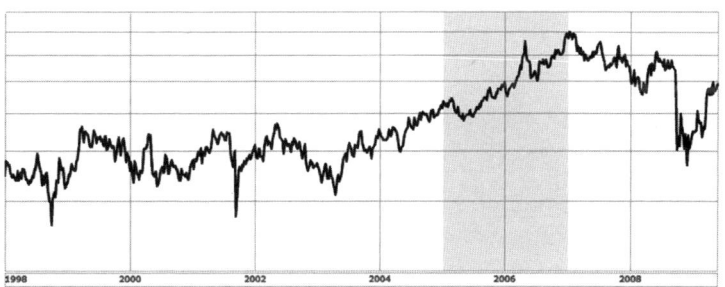

Honda

not Procter & Gamble. The share price of the personal care giant has hit almost $70, up 20% from under $62 a share back in July."[36]

2006 and 2007, the years in which Stengel's Lion-winning campaigns ran, were record years for P&G in terms of business success and stock market performance. Like Volkswagen, they beat the S&P500 and eclipsed their decade average of 4.7% with an 06/07 average of 10.9% share price growth.[37]

At the end of 2006, six months before Cannes crowned Honda their 2007 Advertiser of the Year, the Japanese carmaker hit their highest recorded share price of $38.50.[38] A series of extraordinary campaigns in 2005 and 2006 including 'Cog' and 'Grrr' had driven a turnaround in perceptions toward the Honda brand and a 28% increase in UK sales.[39]

And just like Volkswagen and P&G, Honda's Advertiser of the Year award was preceded by two years of remarkable share performance – growing 24% against a decade average of 4.7% and an S&P500 index of 10.35%.

adidas' 2006 Cannes Advertiser of the Year colours came at the end of a period of 35% share price growth, more than four times the S&P500.[40] Again this was a record result for adidas, following a wave of exceptional creative work. USA sales lifted 11%[41] and the company experienced its most vigorous stock market performance in history.

The year prior, PlayStation won Advertiser of the Year. As a sub-brand of Sony, PlayStation doesn't exist as an independent

The case for creative companies

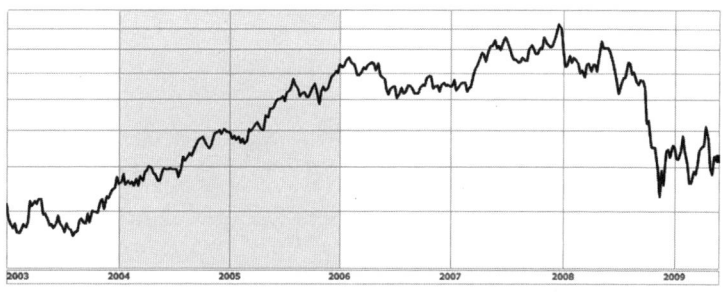

adidas

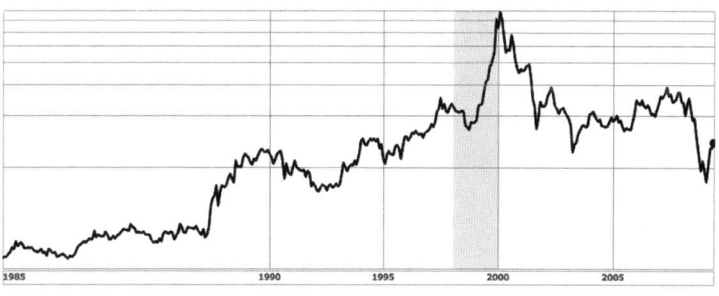

Sony

financial entity and thus there's no stock market performance to report. However, the years leading up to 2005 were instrumental in the PS2 becoming the world's best-selling gaming console, having shifted in excess of 100 million units.[42]

In 2004 BMW received the Advertiser of the Year award for, among other campaigns, the 'BMW Films' campaign out of Fallon. Following a 12% sales increase after the first series of the films,[43] BMW's share price grew 16% in 2003, a huge rally during a turbulent period for the stock market following the events of 9/11.[44]

The ever-bullish Nike, 2003's Advertiser of the Year, didn't let that period hold them back either. "We decided to cross the threshold of September 11," wrote CEO and founder Phil Knight in his 2002 annual report. "Eight months later we delivered a 14% increase in earnings, and beat the S&P by 45 points... a defining moment... a Nike moment."[45]

The 2002 Advertiser of the Year was Swatch. According to the Cannes press release, they'd "consistently produced exciting advertising, including a film lion for 'Swatch Goal Keeper' and a press lion for 'Mosquito' in 1999, a press lion in 2000 for 'Suicide' and in 2001, lions in both press and outdoor for their 'Scuba Collection' campaign."

During that 1999-2001 period, the S&P500 didn't grow a cent. Swatch, however, doubled their share value with one of the steepest periods of stock market growth on record.[46]

Anheuser Busch told the same story the year prior. Just like the others, their 2001 Advertiser of the Year award was preceded by two years of share price rises that beat their decade average and eclipsed the S&P500.[47]

Cannes began the twenty-first century by naming Sony its 2000 Advertiser of the Year. Primarily for TBWA\'s work on PlayStation, the award was given to Sony CEO Nobuyuki Idei.

Sony's 1999 year was extraordinary. The share price increased a staggering 242%, ten times the S&P500 and Sony's decade average. On February 28, 2000, Sony's stock hit an all-time high of $149.72, a figure it's never met since.[48]

"You know, the Procter & Gamble of 15 years ago basically said 'humour has no role in advertising'," remembers Jim Stengel. "Procter & Gamble 15 years ago said 'we'll never go to Cannes'."

He speaks with measured conviction, but his tone still manages to convey how archaic he considers those bygone edicts. In 2001, after 18 years with P&G, Stengel was named Global Marketing Officer. His twin legacies are transforming P&G from archetypal conservative FMCG marketer to highly creative brand builder, and helping almost double P&G's revenue by the time he departed in 2008.

"Back in 2001, the company was in a funk," he says. "The results were not strong. People were not inspired. So when I got into the role I did a lot of talking to our agencies, a lot of talking to our people, I went outside the company a lot and talked to a lot of different people, people I respected in all kinds of industries. I remember talking to Leo Burnett about Michael Conrad's work on creativity back in the nineties.[49] I did some benchmarking myself, I commissioned a very special study to look into companies and brands that grew faster than P&G and what could I learn about them. I looked at what brands within P&G were growing faster. And so I did an awful lot of exploration early in my role, and I worked with my team to say 'okay, what do we want to be here? Are we okay with being an average consumer products company?' Because we had fallen. Our results had really stalled. So we kind of rallied around this idea of being the best. We wanted to be the best in the world. And I'm not sure P&G had ever been that bold. They always wanted to be the best in their category. But we said, you know, versus Apple, versus Nike, versus anyone, we want to be up there. The reputation, results, creativity and people. And we were nowhere close to being that. Not even close. P&G was very left brain, very dogmatic, and the company quite frankly didn't know what to do with the right side of the brain."

Those discussions and benchmarking studies led to P&G thinking very differently about creativity, even to the extent of flying their marketing team to the Cannes festival in 2003 for the first time in the company's history.

"We really raised our standards on creativity. And going to Cannes was a part of that. Going to Cannes was a strong message inside of the company, and outside, that things had changed. That expectations were different, and that we really did want to attract the best talent within our agencies, and have them be as proud of our work as any client in the world. So Cannes was certainly part of that strategy. But it wasn't the only part. You know I got the agencies together for a regular rhythm. I would get Kevin Roberts, Maurice Levy, the head of Leo Burnett which was Linda Wolf at the time, we would get Ed Meyer at Grey, all the heads of our major agencies, and I'd put them in one room for two days. I'd get in front of them and say 'here's what I'm trying to do'. And I'd bring in our CEO and say, 'A.G., just tell them honestly how you're seeing the business, the brands, the people'. And by the way I had the creative heads of each agency. We had Droga in there, we had Isherwood, we had Conrad, we had Mellors, and we put them all in a room and I said 'here's what we're trying to do', and actually we approached it like a team. And out of one of those meetings came the idea to go to Cannes. I brought in a couple of new agencies, because I thought we could learn a lot from them. I brought in Wieden+Kennedy. I brought in TBWA\Chiat\Day. With Gillette we got BBDO. We went to Cannes. We instituted awards. We really changed our standards. We celebrated great creativity in lots of different ways."

Around the same time as Jim Stengel was setting P&G's new creative agenda, BMW and their agency Fallon were enjoying the runaway success of their 'BMW Films' campaign. That work had been the product of a period of soul-searching not unlike P&G's.

"In 1999," says ex-BMW CMO Jim McDowell, "we decided that we wanted to do a major branding effort for BMW. The problem was, every time we saw the work we just weren't satisfied with it. It just didn't seem as though it was making enough of a big brand statement for BMW. Our agency had been making proposals to us for more than a year. Then we said, maybe we're too structured in terms of the way that we approach our brand understanding. We had lots of rules about how you'd project the BMW brand."

Today Jim McDowell is CEO of Mini, another of the world's most creative advertisers. Ten years earlier, he took the decision to challenge some of the conventional wisdom around brand management to allow for much more creative thinking.

"We had very specific perspectives on how BMW needed to be pictured in any kind of television advertising, how they needed to be photographed, what kind of language, tonality we wanted, and we thought maybe the problem with this branding effort is that we just have too many rules."

So they went to Fallon with a new brief. "Give us some ideas where you break one or another of the rules that we've set, so we can see if maybe it's our rules that are hemming you in. So then they came back and said, 'We have an idea, but it's not for television.' And we said okay, so print? And they said 'No, it's not print either.' The idea is to do a series of amazing short films on the internet, and that they'd probably be the most exciting thing that most people had ever seen on their computer screen."

Like Stengel, Jim McDowell's creative ambition was inspired by the behaviour of other very successful companies.

"At both BMW and at Mini, we studied people that had done remarkable things in marketing and tried to figure out how they did it. We studied previous efforts in all sorts of different industries where something had caught on a lot quicker than you would have imagined and why."

"And would you say that those companies behaved in a highly creative way to achieve those successes", I ask him.

"Yeah, I would say that," he tells me.

Creatively focused marketing leaders are clearly something of a precursor to winning Cannes Advertiser of the Year. But the common factor among the Cannes Advertisers of the Year wasn't simply creatively focused marketers, but how those marketers were operating within companies that had a much broader creative agenda. Companies in the thick of periods of increased creativity in everything they did.

Erich Stamminger, adidas' President and CEO, was Head of Global Marketing up until 2006 when he became CEO. One of the architects of 'Impossible is Nothing', he used the creative spirit of that external brand positioning to drive culture and innovation throughout adidas. "For each and every member of the adidas family," he said, "'Impossible is Nothing', this attitude, this philosophy, has become part of our daily lives and our language."

Innovating relentlessly through the early days of 'Impossible is Nothing', adidas launched the adidas_1 – the world's first intelligent shoe, opened their innovative Sports Performance Centre retail stores all over the world, launched Project Fusion, the world's first completely integrated training system, created the +F50 TUNIT – the first modular football boot, and established design partnerships with Stella McCartney and Yohji Yamamoto. Extraordinary growth followed, and across the decade of 'Impossible is Nothing', adidas grew from a €4.6 billion brand to one worth almost €8 billion.[51]

It's a similar story for BMW. "Without a doubt that was a really good period for BMW in the United States," says McDowell. "We had year after year of consecutive growth, and we still continued that pretty well after September 11, 2001. That was a time when people were really unsettled in the United States, and BMW still had pretty robust sales."

That business success coincided with a wider agenda of innovation. "It was a very good period for innovation in the United States for BMW. In the late 1990s, BMW made a lot of changes to their cars to make them just perfect for the US market, and that was something we were benefiting from as we headed into the 2000s. And that effort at BMW led to the first Z3 launch. It was the first time BMW built a two-seat sports car for the mass market. The car was built in South Carolina, and it was introduced as James Bond traded in his Aston Martin for a BMW."

In the case of Volkswagen, their business success accelerated as CEO Martin Winterkorn arrived fresh from completing Audi's design-led renaissance. He came with plans to innovate heavily and grow Volkswagen to replace Toyota as the world's largest automaker.

At Honda, the 'Power of Dreams' campaign built on the imagination and creative passion of founder Sochiro Honda and engineer Kenichi Nagahiro, who completely recreated the diesel engine for Honda.

In the case of Swatch, Cannes made specific mention of founder and CEO Nicolas Hayek's imaginative spirit. "This honour recognises the creative and innovative talents demonstrated by Mr Hayek, be it in Swatch product development or in Swatch advertising." Besides making the world's most creative watches, Hayek also created the Smart Car, in a joint venture with Mercedes-Benz, and served as member of a number of high-profile European government councils aimed at developing strategies for stimulating innovations for the future.

Sony and Nike persist in prioritising creativity and innovation. "The trouble in America is not that we are making too many mistakes," advises Nike CEO Phil Knight on innovation, "but that we are making too few."

"You know, we'd been through the dark ages," says Stengel of P&G, "and then we had the enlightenment. A.G. Lafley {P&G's CEO at the time} was a wonderful leader and he pretty much said to all of us, you know, I want all of us to create, to innovate, to think differently. He said to the R&D head, 'We think we know better than everyone else. We think we have the best scientists, you know, 1,100 PhDs, we have 25,000 patents, blah blah blah.' He said, 'Well, you know, there are a lot of people outside this company who are really smart. What if half of our innovation could be sourced from outside the company? I'd like you to try that. And I'd like you to measure it.' So of course that totally disrupted how they worked. And all of a sudden we'd developed these internet-based platforms where we'd put problems out and have scientists in Russia and China and India solve them. And A.G. was famous for saying, 'We've gone from 1,100 R&D people to, like, 12 million, and didn't raise our overheads!'"

P&G didn't just become more creative in its advertising, it became more creative in *everything* it did.

"It was a period where we made design much more important, we named a head of design, we put design people on our R&D teams, we contracted with the world's best design firms, people like Ideo. We would do management meetings in design firms. In research we got more interesting, we stopped doing a lot of silly research where you look backwards, we did a lot more experiential research where we got ourselves involved. We would spend a week in a village studying a problem. Sometimes we'd put teams away for three months immersed in a brand restage. It was a period of great innovation across the company, and advertising was part of that."

"People were saying in the early 2000s, this company is as big as it's going to get, where else can they go?" Stengel concludes with a pen portrait of the results of P&G's creative agenda. "We doubled our size. We went from about $43 billion to about $83 billion in basically seven years. Our margins went up ten points. We went from nine billion-dollar brands to 25. And our earnings per share went up fourfold. So, you know, fantastic. Like double, you know, there was no question about the results."

The Cannes Advertiser of the Year award is all about creative advertising, "presented to advertisers who have distinguished themselves for inspiring innovative marketing of their products and who embrace and encourage the creative work produced by their agencies."

In every case, the companies that have been most tenacious in their pursuit of great creativity in their advertising have been among the ones outperforming the stock market and enjoying historic periods of financial prosperity.

And in every case, the leaders of those companies had created a culture of innovation that advertising creativity was symptomatic of, but which extended well beyond advertising and into the culture, the product, the very day-to-day activities of those companies. A creative day-to-day that produced the most extraordinary results in the history of some of the world's most illustrious companies.

8. The future case for creativity

THE CASE FOR CREATIVITY

"It's the future and there's no getting around it. People want to know what other people like them think."

Craig Stoll
Pizzeria Delfina, San Francisco

It just might have been the world's most ingenuous welcome, but it took diners at San Francisco's Pizzeria Delfina a moment to fathom the phrase "This place sucks" printed in large and ultra-readable type on the waitress's t-shirt.

Another staffer's read, "The pizza was soooo greasy. I am assuming this was in part due to the pig fat."

We might have mistaken those words for the artful uprising of an aggrieved staff, but in fact they were the views of an even more turbulent dissenter: the dissatisfied customer who'd shared their judgement on the internet.

In 2009, in a move as intriguing as it was confronting, the management at Pizzeria Delfina lifted the cruellest reviews of

THE CASE FOR CREATIVITY

Workers at Pizzeria Delfina

their establishment from yelp.com, a popular American consumer reviews website, and printed them on the t-shirts their staff wore while they made pizza and served customers.[52]

Rather than burying their heads in the sand and hoping the detractors of their business would disappear, Delfina chose to brave them head on. They brought criticism out into the open, giving themselves a unique way to engage customers and turn negative online comments into positive real world conversations.

It's a fascinating example of one business's reaction to the explosion of conversations about products and brands that are being had, and listened into, by today's connected consumers. Those conversations are a phenomenon that's having a dramatic effect on how we decide which products to buy and which brands to align ourselves with.

Creating word of mouth has always been something of a novelty aspiration for agencies and their campaigns. Whether it was 'water cooler chat' about last night's TVC in the 90s, or in more recent times having your experiential campaign blogged about, there's been a huge caché among creative folk for stuff that gets discussed by consumers and the media.

However, it hasn't been until now that we've been able to quantify the value of campaigns that create conversation.

"Those campaigns that get talked about a lot," say the

authors of *Marketing in the Era of Accountability*, "the ones we call 'fame' campaigns – they're the most effective of all. They're conspicuously the most effective campaigns out there.

"'Fame' campaigns work by getting the brand talked about and generally making it more famous. This is not the same thing as saying the advertising is designed to raise brand awareness (which most advertising seeks to do) – it is about creating perceptions of being the brand that is 'making waves'. These campaigns often generate strong emotional responses in the target group (not necessarily liking) and so cause the brand to stand out distinctly from other brands in the category. They usually become talked about not in a functional way, but by virtue of the attitudes and point of view they project for the brand. This encourages brand usage by creating perceptions that the brand is bigger and 'more important' than before."

This wasn't merely conjecture. The IPA's analysis of the 880 available marketing case histories showed that those campaigns that achieved 'fame' achieved an effectiveness success rate significantly higher than campaigns that were simply emotional in their content, persuasive in their argument or rational in their messaging. More than any other kind of campaign, 'fame' campaigns drove very large effects on hard business measures such as sales, market share or profit.

Three years later, the IPA report 'The Link Between Creativity and Effectiveness' found a distinct correlation between creatively-awarded campaigns and levels of 'fame'.

"The most significant difference between creatively-awarded and non-awarded campaigns was in the scale of the fame effects they generated, i.e. online and offline buzz. Creatively-awarded campaigns were twice as likely to generate very large fame effects than non-awarded campaigns."

The study went on to make the astute observation that while you can buy awareness, you can't buy fame. That awareness (which correlates very loosely with effectiveness) is dependent on money, while fame (which correlates very tightly with effectiveness) is dependent on *creativity*.

If fame has been that critical to effectiveness in the past, it will almost certainly become more so in the future. To understand why, let's travel back to the middle of the 1990s, to the genesis of a curious occurrence known as Corporate Social Responsibility (CSR) Marketing.

There was no fashion among the 80s business person for responsibility. No pressure to set profits aside for the benevolent support of a charitable cause, to reduce the environmental impact of their product, to improve the nutritional value of their snack foods. They were simple times for capitalism.

But by the middle of the 90s, ideas like 'good corporate citizenship' and 'triple bottom line accounting' were becoming popularised, and as they gained ground, a generation of sensitive new-age marketers began to spend their budgets telling people just how earnestly their company was approaching its social responsibilities.

"Trust us," the advertisements implored, "we're doing the right thing."

By the middle of the 2000s the fashion had become a table stake and almost every advertiser in the world was at some point communicating their environmental, nutritional or charitable good-doing to their customers.

There was a sudden epidemic of business benevolence, supported by an influx of billions of dollars of marketing spend to tell everybody. So how much better are consumers feeling about businesses as a result?

Researcher and social trend analyst Daniel Yankelovich periodically polls consumers with the question, "Do you trust businesspeople to do the right thing most or all of the time?"

In the middle of the 90s, the majority said they trusted businesspeople. Soon after, that level of trust began to drop. By 2002, just 36% of people said they trusted businesspeople. It fell further to 32% in 2004, then to 28% in 2006.[53] The World Economic Forum corroborated Yankelovich's findings when in their 2005 global survey they found trust in corporations to be at its lowest level since tracking began.[54]

On a graph, the trust consumers show in corporates is inversely proportionate to the amount of money being spent by those corporates attempting to earn consumers' trust. Not only has our CSR spend produced no lift in consumer trust, it appears to have exacerbated its decline!

This reality is a provocative one for marketers, whose communications budgets are largely spent according to the idea that if you send a positive message about your product or company out into the marketplace, and it reaches the right people, that this will have a positive effect on the way those people feel about you. That by and large, people hear marketing messages, and believe marketing messages.

But if that were the case, all those unreservedly positive CSR messages would have to have produced some effect. The truth is they've had none.

Once upon a time, however, they would have had. Marketing's belief in firing messages at consumers is founded in decades of successful twentieth-century 'bigger, faster, brighter' advertising. But something's changed. People are still forming opinions of products and companies, but today it's something besides marketing messages that's influencing them.

In 2007 *Business Week* journalist David Armano suggested that we're moving from an 'attention economy' to a 'conversation economy'.[55] That the emergence of digital technologies like mobile phones and the internet has enabled us to spend more time, having more conversations, with more people than ever before. He warned that this phenomenon came with implications for marketers and businesses.

His thinking was based on research like that of Fleishman Hillard's 'Digital Influence Index', which tracks the amount of time that consumers around the world spend with various media each week.[56]

It tracks those traditional media that marketers have historically used to fire messages at consumers – TV, radio, newspapers, magazines. And it tracks those new media – the internet, email and mobile phones – which facilitate conversations between consumers.

Before this century, our media time was obviously dominated by the traditional options. But in 2010, the report shows that while we're spending 23.3 hours per week with TV, newspapers, radio and magazines, we're spending 24.1 hours with the internet, email, mobile phones and having good old-fashioned real world conversations with our friends and family.

That research isn't saying traditional media is dead. What it is saying is that in the past we *predominantly* spent our time receiving messages, whereas today we *predominantly* spend our time having conversations. Be it via TXT, Facebook, Twitter, blog commentary, Instant Messenger, email, or simply a phone call, conversing has become our number one pastime.

And naturally, with so many conversations happening, some of them are going to be about companies and their products.

A Twitter search of 'Vodafone' throws up a seemingly endless stream of tweets about the global telco. "Dear Vodafone," says one, "your services are constantly unavailable. You suck." Another reads "I'm quite impressed with Vodafone. Just had a one-hour conversation to Lagos on less than €5 credit."

On yelp.com, the aforementioned consumer reviews website, people air their views of every conceivable kind of company or service. Started in San Francisco in 2004, the website has achieved prodigious popularity and is in the process of being rolled out to the rest of the world's large cities. San Francisco local 'John F' may not have perfect English, but his opinion of the McDonalds on Stanyan Street is accorded the same opportunity as anyone's in Yelp's democratic process. "This McDonald is hella dirty," he observes, "there is always a drug dealer hanging at the bus stop to sell drug to the lazy hippies. Their bathroom is dirty, and sometime out of order because of the hobos."

Linguistic innovation aside, John isn't unusual. In 2007 a global study by advertising network McCann Erickson sought to understand how many people regularly share their views of companies and products online. The findings were extraordinary, showing that in the past month over 40% of those surveyed had discussed a product or service over Instant Messenger or email, and that over a quarter had recommended or condemned a product or service on a blog, social network site, or consumer reviews site.[57]

Facebook groups are created in honour of well-loved products (here in New Zealand, the 'When they got rid of Grapefruit & Lemon Frujus I died a little inside' group inspired local ice cream company Tip Top to bring back a well-loved ice lolly [58]) and YouTube clips vividly capture poor service experiences (the video showing a Comcast cable installer asleep on a customer's couch after dozing off halfway through the job [59]).

The disparities between the messages that companies put in their advertising and the actual cleanliness of their corporate washing are easily accessible today. It takes under a minute to find Coke's 'Happiness Factory' advertisement and contrast it with an abundance of news articles with titles like 'Coca Cola: drinking the world dry'.[60]

And not only has the truth been democratised, it's also been search engine optimised. A recent UK study found that 40% of the top 50 UK brands' Google pages feature negative PR.[61] Many of the top ten results returned after Googling those brands were stories that conflicted with the positive messages being sent out by their marketing departments.

That's a scary fact when, for many companies, Google *is* their homepage. In 2010, 30 times more people Googled 'Ford' than visited ford.com.[62] Their heavily sanitised corporate website full of positive messages is all a bit academic when Google points people first to consumer generated content on Wikipedia and Jeremy Clarkson's frank reviews of Ford's products on YouTube.

Compounding this issue is consumers' increasing propensity to trust what they hear from their peers more than what they hear from marketing.

Mike Hutcheson, one of the founders of the agency where I work, tells a story about the family of Hylton Mackley, another of the founders. He shows a very old ad for a car called an 'Essex Super Six'. "This is a story about Hylton's uncle, Garnett Hercules Mackley," says Mike. "He bought this Essex Super Six back in 1937 or whenever it was, and his wife asked him, 'Why did you buy that, my dear?' and he said, 'Well they speak very well of it in the advertisements'."

Gone are such innocent days. Forrester Research recently showed that up until 2002, 78% of consumers said advertising was a good way to find out about new products. In the four years that followed, that figure dropped to 52%. Over the same period, the people who agreed that 'companies generally tell the truth in ads' dropped from 13% to just 6%.[63] That 6% is a particularly low figure, but still, most equivalent trust studies show that these days at best a quarter of people believe what they hear in advertising, whereas between 50% and 80% believe what they hear from a friend or peer.

And by 'peer', people increasingly mean 'others like me' as opposed to people they actually know. Strangers' reviews on websites and comments on Facebook are more believable than a message from a brand that's been in your pantry since you were a kid.

That's the reason why CSR marketing is such a squanderous pursuit. People hear the positive messages. But they also hear conflicting messages in the conversations they have and listen in to. And, forced to make a choice, they believe the conversations.

THE CASE FOR CREATIVITY

Susan Boyle

Today people's perceptions of products and companies are being shaped more and more by conversations and less and less by marketing messages.

It isn't comforting news. For most of us, the prospect of relinquishing the safety blanket of ads containing positive messages is a frightening one. Messages are easy. We understand how to choose them and how to communicate them.

Though the process of starting and shaping conversations seems at first to be overwhelming, as if entering into a battle with chaos theory itself, we can gather a modest education from a handful of companies that seem to have uncovered the first principles of How To Do It.

The darlings of the conversation economy of the 2000s were consumer technology innovations like Toyota's Prius, Apple's iPhone, Nintendo's Wii and the TiVo. We naturally wonder what it is about these inventions that have people conversing so fervently.

The answer may lie in the unlikely success of Susan Boyle, one of the biggest conversations of the century thus far. Who didn't find themselves talking about Susan Boyle in the weeks following her appearance on 'Britain's Got Talent'? Ms Boyle gave a wonderful performance, but we didn't talk about her for that reason. We did so because she completely shattered the category conventions of pop stardom. She's an old hairy lady. We talked about her because she's surprising. She's different. She's *interesting*.

When the aforementioned Howard Gossage said, "Nobody reads advertising. People read what interests them, and sometimes it's an ad," he was speaking in the 1950s of the importance of creativity in print advertising. But if he were alive today, I'm sure he'd say something like, "Nobody talks about brands. People talk about what interests them, and sometimes it's a brand."

The thing that the Prius, the iPhone, the Wii and the TiVo have in common is their *interestingness*. They each perform their set task brilliantly well. That's important. We wouldn't have talked about Susan Boyle if her singing was average. But functional brilliance alone doesn't get talked about. The Prius is a great car, but also an interesting car. It's a hybrid. It's a funny shape. It's surprising. And for that reason it's worth having a conversation about. The iPhone is completely different from every phone that came before it. You use the Wii in a completely different way to a PlayStation or xBox. The TiVo allows you to watch television in a completely different way. They're all interesting. They're all unlike anything else. And so they're all worth talking about.

A less familiar example can be found in the story of USA cleaning products manufacturer Method. They make supermarket products with which to sanitise your dishes, your shower door or your floorboards. Their products work extremely well. But they're also completely different from anything else available.

Method was formed to create cleaning products that have no impact on the environment. It sounds a hackneyed raison d'etre these days, but Method's interestingness is in their execution. Explaining his company's desire not to make a toilet bowl cleaner unless it was non-toxic enough to drink, CEO Eric Ryan actually imbibed from a bottle of his Lil' Bowl Blue toilet product at a launch press conference.[64] Showing no less respect for plant life, their all-purpose cleaner has been proven to be able to sustain a flower in the same way a vase of water would. Method is one of the world's most talked about brands, and was one of the last decade's fastest growing American companies.[65]

In exploring such colourful examples, it's difficult not to consider the interestingness of the products our own company creates. For many of us, they fall short of the high water mark set by the likes of Method. But as conversations become ever more influential in our purchasing decisions, interestingness will become an increasingly consequential measure in the process of product innovation.

Reassuringly, there's solace for those of us who preside over currently uninteresting products. In the same way interesting product ideas can create conversations, interesting marketing ideas can have a similar effect.

German football boot company Nomis sells its boots in a truly interesting way. From its store in Berlin, you're fitted and sent away with just one boot, for your right foot. No money is

THE CASE FOR CREATIVITY

Method's Lil' Bowl Blu toilet bowl cleaner

exchanged, just an agreement that you'll wear the right boot alongside your existing left one, and after two weeks, if you like the Nomis boot better you'll be charged and sent the matching leftie.[66] Imagine the chatter upon taking the field in mismatched footwear. The interestingness of this idea makes it highly contagious.

In 2008 Australia's Four n' Twenty pies ran a hilarious promotion during which, for the price of $5 and two barcodes, you'd be sent the Magic Salad Plate. A simple white dish onto which has been glued a fake plastic salad, this ingenious creation relieves men of the weight of society's expectation that they eat more healthily. 'Have a lunch that's edible on a plate that's credible,' the advertising tells Aussie blokes. After selling thousands of plates, pie sales grew 30% – an unprecedented result which followed a delightful conversation rather than a clumsy attempt to send consumers a 'unique selling proposition' about Four n' Twenty pies.[67]

Here in New Zealand, one of the biggest conversations in recent marketing history was the Yellow Pages Group's 'Treehouse Restaurant' campaign. To demonstrate the power of their product, Yellow challenged unknown accordian player Tracey Collins to build a restaurant halfway up a redwood pine tree using only contacts from the Yellow book, website and mobile application. In January 2009, the Treehouse opened to a sellout season, feeding 2,000 diners from around the world. A delightful example of a brand letting its actions speak louder

THE CASE FOR CREATIVITY

Four 'n Twenty's Magic Salad Plate

than its words, the interestingness of the Treehouse bewitched consumers and the media alike, spreading through the conversations of 20,000 websites, 100 global magazines, every major national television news property, the front page of the *New Zealand Herald* (our country's biggest daily newspaper) and even the blog of Kanye West. The impact of those conversations was a measurable public reassessment of the Yellow brand and a share increase in online lookups at the expense of Google, an opponent previously dismissed as unassailable. The fact that only US$250,000 was spent on advertising media – a relatively miniscule budget for a major brand like Yellow – serves as evidence that it was the conversations, not messages and paid media, that created the result. In recognition of its efficacy, the campaign received the Platinum award at the 2009 Asia Pacific Marketing Effectiveness Awards – the decoration given to the most effective marketing effort from a pool of nearly six hundred 2008 campaigns from India to New Zealand.[68]

In the words of Craig Stoll, owner of Pizzeria Delfina, "it's the future, and there's no getting around it... people want to know what other people like them think."[69] They want to talk to each other about their experiences with products and brands, and they want to form their view based on those conversations, creating a clear need for brands to do whatever they can to be worth talking about. One of the most efficient ways

being to use advertising creativity to create 'fame'.

'Fame' campaigns, both in the anecdotal successes and in the broad based analyses, punch well above their weight with regard to short-term sales gains. But Peter Field believes there's another even more beneficial effect of creating conversation.

"The real benefit of these campaigns," he says, "the ones that generate the strong word of mouth response – and the data seems to support this – is not just in the volume sales result, but in the price sensitivity and price elasticity of brands. To cut a long story short, people are prepared to pay more for the brands that people talk about, people just feel better about parting with their money for those kinds of brands. An extra percent of volume, only a small proportion of that is profit. Whereas if you raise your price by 1%, essentially all of that is incremental profit, it goes straight to the bottom line. So the price sensitivity benefit of fame advertising is that it not only helps with volume but also with value and that's really important."

In a conversation economy, uncreative advertising becomes even less effective than it was in the old 'attention economy'. People talk only about things that interest them, and the fact is that rationally based, uncreative advertising is very rarely 'interesting' to anybody. And while awareness can be bought, awareness doesn't translate into conversation without the crucial ingredient of creativity.

Creativity creates conversation, which builds value into brands, which in turn creates financial success. Every day we become more of a conversation economy. And so if there has proved to be a strong case for creativity in the past, that case will only be stronger in the future.

9. The case for creativity

"By the way, if anyone here is in advertising or marketing, kill yourself."

Bill Hicks

The case for creativity

Creativity is good for business.

It makes companies more successful by making their advertising far more effective in delivering a return on their investment.

The 15 industry and academic studies covered in this book represent two decades of research comparing the effects of a more creative approach with a less creative one. They represent not only a correlation between more creative advertising and more effective advertising, but also a deep understanding of exactly *how* creativity makes advertising more effective – from making it stand out more, to making it more likely to be recalled, to getting it talked about more and finally to making it more persuasive.

What makes the case all the more compelling is the absence

of contrary research. If there is a case *against* creativity, it's extremely difficult to find. I've never seen a study that concludes that a less creative approach is a more effective one. Every one of the dozens of university academics and industry professionals who have explored this topic has arrived at the same conclusion.

The wonderful thing about creativity is that it isn't only good for business.

It's also good for *people*.

The same is difficult to say for advertising in general.

"Advertising is a racket," said F. Scott Fitzgerald. "You cannot be honest without admitting that its constructive contribution to humanity is exactly minus zero."

Even advertising legend David Ogilvy sympathised. "As a private person," he said, "I have a passion for landscape, and I have never seen one improved by a billboard. When I retire from Madison Avenue, I am going to start a secret society of masked vigilantes who will travel around the world on silent motorbicycles, chopping down posters at the dark of the moon. How many juries will convict us when we are caught in these acts of beneficent citizenship?"

And it's something of an irony that Bill Hicks, the American comedian who's among the most adored by advertising creatives, is perhaps their most vehement detractor.

"By the way, if anyone here is in advertising or marketing," he famously ranted on stage in the early 1990s, "Kill yourself. Seriously though, if you are, do. You think there's going to be a joke coming. There's no joke coming. You are Satan's spawn, filling the world with bile and garbage. Kill yourself."

Hicks' tongue was sharper than most, but his views aren't necessarily extreme. A recent study showed that 65% of consumers feel "constantly bombarded" with advertising and that 60% have a "much more negative opinion towards advertising than they did a few years ago".[70]

Far be it from me to suggest that we have any sort of responsibility to *not* fill the world with bile and garbage. (As Howard Gossage once said, "to explain responsibility to advertising men is like trying to convince an eight-year-old that sexual intercourse is more fun than a chocolate ice cream cone.")

But in fact, electing to keep the advertising landscape beautiful mightn't be quite the hippie ideology that it sounds. Gallup & Robinson recently found that consumers who felt better about advertising in general tended to recall and be persuaded by specific advertisements more than those with negative attitudes toward advertising.[71] What they showed was that if we improve the overall palatability of advertising, we'll improve the ROI we see on our advertising spend. So it's very much in our commercial interests not to fill the world with bile and garbage.

And furthermore, isn't it brilliant when we can achieve

success for our clients while at the same time contributing something of value to the world around us?

And I don't mean CSR marketing. I mean creativity.

When we produced the 'Treehouse Restaurant' campaign for Yellow Pages Group, we anticipated a campaign that would garner media attention and make a difference to our client's business. It did that in droves, but what we hadn't anticipated was just how much consumers who engaged with the campaign would get out of it. While the restaurant was open, we were inundated with notes from consumers who'd eaten their dinner inside our ad campaign and had the time of their lives doing it.

"We ate at the Treehouse on the 17th," wrote one diner, "and the whole evening was magical from start to finish. It was a unique experience that will never be forgotten. Thank you."

"What a fabulous experience," said another. "The food was fantastic, the service brilliant – and the location, well, a once in a lifetime experience."

A third had her birthday in the tree. "We feel it was a privilege to be able to come and visit the place. Thank you for making our day so perfect and the start of my 50th year something extra special."

The Yellow Treehouse wasn't a social marketing campaign, or a charity campaign, or a campaign for another 'good cause'. It was a regular old 'selling' campaign for a commercial organisation wanting more people to use its products. And yet it managed to make that happen without filling the world with more bile and garbage.

Making advertising's great. Making advertising that works, even better. But making advertising that works while at the same time contributing something of value to the world... would even Bill Hicks approve?

Or, more pertinently, would consumers feel better about those companies that chose to advertise without the bile and garbage?

Agnosticism notwithstanding, my favourite quote of all time comes from a thirteenth-century French Roman Catholic friar by the name of St Francis of Assisi.

"Preach the Gospel at all times," he counselled his *fratres*. "Use words if necessary."

His insight was that people infer things about you not only from what you *say*, but also from what you *do* and how you do it. That there is *unspoken* communication, and that others often pay more attention to this than they do to the words we speak.

It took 750 years for behavioural psychology to catch up with St Francis, but in 1967, three American psychologists found that "what they termed metacommunication (i.e. the non-verbal emotive paraphernalia which accompanies what was being said) was far more potent at influencing interpersonal

THE CASE FOR CREATIVITY

St Francis of Assisi

relationships than the content of the communication. In simple terms, changing what people said had little influence on how they felt about one another, but changing how they said it had a big influence."[72]

It's as true for advertising as it is for any form of communication. Research has shown that consumers' outtakes of advertising are formed not only by the message in the advertising, but also by the variables of how that message is delivered.

For example, how much money is spent on delivering it.

"Advertising expense is an indicator of marketing effort," wrote a small tweed of academics from the Stockholm School of Economics in 2008. "The more money spent on advertising, the greater the effort, meaning that the advertiser must really believe in the product. Spending a great deal of money on advertising is a more powerful signal to consumers about the quality of the product than the content of the advertising, as the advertiser has 'put their money where their mouth is'. More money means greater risk, and thus consumers feel safe that the advertiser will deliver on their promise."

Intrigued by the effects of the unspoken, those academics went on to publish a groundbreaking study on another form of unspoken communication – creativity.

"We expect that greater creativity signals more effort (as creative advertising is harder to produce) and thus produces more favorable brand perceptions."

They hypothesised that beyond helping a message stand out

and persuade, creativity had yet another positive effect. That Companies that went to the trouble of being creative would be thought better of by consumers.

They studied over 1,200 people aged 18 to 65, showing them both creative and uncreative advertising, and then measuring the differences in how that advertising made them feel about the companies being advertised.

The findings were extraordinary. They discovered that more creative advertising, regardless of whether the creativity was at all relevant to the selling message, had a far greater impact than less creative advertising on consumers' positive perceptions of the company being advertised.

Compared with less creative advertising for the same company, the more creative advertising made people conclude that the company had gone to a greater effort for them (52% higher for creative advertising), that the company was smarter (69% higher), that the company developed more valuable products (50% higher), that the company was better at solving problems (83% higher), that the company's products were of a higher quality (36% higher), that the company was worthy of their interest (88% higher), and that the company's products were worth purchasing (73% higher).[73]

When we choose to be more creative with our advertising, we don't just improve its chances of communicating its message. We send a second and perhaps even louder message to consumers that we're a smarter company with better products.

A company that takes pride in the things it does and strives for excellence. When we choose to be less creative, we communicate the opposite. One wonders how many well-intentioned messages have gone to waste having been out-shouted by uncreative delivery.

As this book went to print, creative award shows around the world were evolving to reflect an even greater interest in advertising effectiveness, encouraging creative people toward work that's both creative *and* effective.

The One Show has announced that from 2010 onwards, it will penalise any agency that enters ads proven to have been conceived primarily for awards, rather than for the commercial gain of their client.

Cannes have taken an approach of incentivisation rather than penalty by introducing the Creative Effectiveness Lions. This new part of the week at Cannes recognises those campaigns that were creative enough to win a shortlist place or better at Cannes, and also achieved extraordinary business results. What's more, the Creative Effectiveness Lions will be awarded on Cannes' Saturday night show with the Film and Titanium & Integrated Lions, positioning them alongside the most prestigious categories to win in at Cannes.

No doubt, these developments are in part a response to the cynicism stirred up when ineffective campaigns are given awards.

Creative award shows are well known to celebrate campaigns that don't go on to win effectiveness awards. For many, it's a sore point and throws the legitimacy of creative awards into question. Why would we award campaigns on any basis other than their effectiveness? Advertising's got one job, and that's to sell stuff. If it doesn't, then what does it matter how 'creative' it is?

Effectiveness awards have a more apparent value. They celebrate the prosperity of our clients and help us understand what leads to significant success. But while effectiveness award shows tend to be dominated by big campaigns for big brands with big media budgets, creative award shows tend to be the opposite. They're usually dominated by smaller campaigns, often for smaller brands, and usually with smaller media allocations.

The reason for this, of course, is that when there's less to lose, clients are willing to be more creative. It's the campaign for the pro-bono client that had production and media resources donated. It's the campaign for the large corporate's smallest product line. It's the single maverick execution among a much bigger and less creative campaign. It's the fringes.

At creative award shows we celebrate the bleeding edge of experimentalism, of entrepreneurialism, of innovation in advertising. And the fringes are usually where agencies do their most innovative work, because those fringes are where clients feel most comfortable taking the greatest risks.

An unfortunate side effect is that effectiveness is rarely

measured at the fringes. Large campaigns for large brands get measured. The client has funding and systems in place for measurement, and a need to prove the return on such a large investment. Measurement, being an expensive exercise, is rarely affordable for small campaigns or small brands, and as a campaign gets smaller, isolating its effects from everything else going on in the market becomes exponentially more difficult and expensive.

With adequate resourcing we might find that those small, award-winning campaigns are in fact highly effective. After all, lack of an Effie isn't evidence that a campaign has been ineffective. But alas, in most cases we're doomed never to know.

The ingrained logic tells us that we're best not to risk it. Why ask the agency for a highly creative campaign and risk it not working when you could ask them for a less creative one and have a surer shot at success?

However, two decades of research shows this to be a misconception, and one that makes ineffective advertising all too common. Each year, we choose to be uncreative most of the time, and we choose to spend more money on those uncreative campaigns than we do on the creative ones. Those campaigns go on to be, on average, much less effective than the creatively awarded ones. And because we've spent more money on them, return on marketing investment is seriously diminished.

The theory that taking a less creative approach is more likely to produce a business result is wrong. There is simply

THE CASE FOR CREATIVITY

no evidence to support that notion, and plenty to disprove it.

It's true that, among the hundreds of thousands of campaigns produced worldwide each year, examples exist of creatively awarded campaigns being ineffective. But while we earnestly try to lessen those instances, it's important to remember just how tremendously uncommon they are.

The research shows that for every 50,000 campaigns, just one will win a creative award without producing a business

---

FOR EVERY 50,000 ADVERTISING CAMPAIGNS PRODUCED:

7	**49,993**
will achieve a creative award	will not achieve a creative award
6	**34,995**
will achieve both a creative award and, on average, a larger business result	will not achieve a creative award, but will achieve, on average, a smaller business result
1	**14,998**
will achieve a creative award but not a business result	will achieve neither a creative award nor a business result

(1 in 7,000 campaigns produced achieve a creative award[74], advertising in general has been shown to achieve a business result 70% of the time[75], and creatively-awarded advertising has been shown to achieve a business result 84% of the time[76])

result. By contrast, just shy of 15,000 uncreative campaigns will deliver no return to their advertiser. And the 34,995 uncreative campaigns that do succeed will be measurably less effective than their creatively awarded counterparts.

Highly creative but ineffective work is extremely rare, but very noticeable because it wins awards.

What's less noticeable, but without doubt of far greater cost to the business community, is the amount of *uncreative* advertising that creates little return on its investment. We're bombarded with it every day of our lives. It's the advertising we've grown so capable of tuning out of that we don't even notice anymore. The 2,998 ads that you can't recall from the last 24 hours. Clients of our industry spend billions of dollars on them each year.

Call me crazy, but shouldn't that be the problem we're working to solve?

Appendix: The 15 Studies

The question of whether a more creative approach is a more effective one has been asked by dozens of people from industry insiders and university academics to the likes of McKinsey & Company. The studies span two decades and are from all corners of the world. They ask the same question, but in 15 different ways. And every one reaches the same conclusion. These are the studies that constitute The Case for Creativity:

1. Creative Advertising and the Von Restorff Effect
Published in *Psychological Reports*, 1991

In which psychologists Pick, Sweeney and Clay show that creativity enhances consumers' unaided recall of advertising.

2. On Resonance: A Critical Pluralistic Inquiry into Advertising Rhetoric
Published in *Journal of Consumer Research*, 1992

In which McQuarrie and Mick show that creativity in the form of word play, ambiguity and incongruity increases liking for the ad, improves brand attitude, and increases unaided recall.

3. Creativity vs Effectiveness? An Integrating Classification for Advertising

Published in *Journal of Advertising Research*, 1995

In which Kover, Goldberg & James of Fordham University, New York, show that creativity facilitates and increases purchase intention, and that campaigns that work at an emotional level are more effective than those that appeal rationally.

4. Do Award-winning Commercials Sell?

Published by Leo Burnett, 1996

In which Donald Gunn shows creatively awarded campaigns to be effective in 86.5% of cases. This study was repeated in 2002, with a result of 82% effectiveness.

5. Recall, Liking and Creativity in TV Commercials: A New Approach

Published in *Journal of Advertising Research*, 2000

In which Stone, Besser and Lewis of Southern Illinois University show well-liked advertising to be much more likely to be creative, and conclude that "there is a much better chance of breaking through the clutter with a creative offering".

6. Breaking Through the Clutter: Benefits of Advertisement Originality and Familiarity for Brand Attention and Memory

Published in *Management Science*, 2002

In which Pieters, Warlop & Wedel of Tilburg University, The Netherlands, show that more original advertising commands greater attention and achieves greater recall.

7. Recall & Persuasion: Does Creative Advertising Matter?

Published in *Journal of Advertising*, 2005

In which Till & Baack, of the University of South Carolina, USA, show that creatively awarded advertising is much more likely to be recalled than advertising in general.

8. Marketing in the Era of Accountability

Published by the IPA, 2007

In which Binet & Field show that campaigns that appeal to the emotions and drive word of mouth are the most effective.

9. Art Meets Science: Creative Advertising Examined

Published in *Power Brands: Measuring, Making, and Managing Brand Success*, 2007

In which McKinsey & Company consultants Hajo Riesenbeck and Jesko Perrey show that more creative campaigns are effective more often than less creative campaigns.

10. The Impact of Advertising Creativity on the Hierarchy of Effects

Published in *Journal of Advertising*, 2008

In which Smith, Chen and Yang of the Universities of Indiana and Wisconsin-Milwaukee show that creative ads attract more attention, create more brand awareness, aid with depth of processing, are more memorable, and most interestingly, reduce consumers' resistance to persuasion.

11. Advertising Creativity Matters

Published in *Journal of Advertising Research*, 2008

In which Dahlén, Rosengren and Törn of the Stockholm School of Economics show that creative advertising makes consumers think better of the companies that produce that advertising.

12. Creative = Effective

Published in *Campaign Brief*, 2008, and repeated in 2011 for Chapter Two of this book.

In which James Hurman shows that creatively focused agencies more efficiently produce more effective advertising.

13. Beyond Attention Effects: Modelling the Persuasive and Emotional Effects of Advertising Creativity

Published in *Marketing Science*, 2009

In which Yang & Smith of the Universities of Wisconsin-Milwaukee and Indiana show that highly creative advertising triggers greater open-mindedness, making consumers more willing to buy, as opposed to be cynical about, the marketing message contained within the advertising.

14. Creative = Successful

Published in *NZ Marketing*, 2010, and expanded on for Chapter Seven of this book.

In which James Hurman shows that the Cannes Advertisers of the Year 2000-2009 all experienced extraordinary sharemarket performances during the period of their Cannes Lion-winning advertising.

15. The Link Between Creativity and Effectiveness

Published by the IPA, 2010

In which Peter Field shows that creative award-winning campaigns are significantly more effective than non-creative-award-winning campaigns.

The point of this book is to share with you the discoveries made in those studies. And for you in turn to be able to share them with others. To help that along, there's a short presentation of the main points available at thecaseforcreativity.com – with any luck it's a practical way to illustrate the value of creativity to those around us, be they advertising people, marketers, or folks from any other walk of business life.

Download it, cut it up, add bits in, pass it off as your own work, whatever does it for you. Find a way to use it to make better, more creative, more effective advertising.

– James Hurman, April 2011

Notes

CHAPTER ONE

[1] Couzens & Ingram's 'Wicked Sick Project' (carried out at George Patterson Y&R Melbourne) was tidily and entertainingly summarised in a case study video that can be found at http://www.youtube.com/watch?v=Cd6-n7MhVg8

[2] J. Walker Smith, president of the consulting firm Yankelovich, told *USA Today* in 2006 that the average 1970s city dweller was exposed to 500 to 2,000 ad messages a day, and that now it's 3,000 to 5,000. For several more thought-provoking statistics on the saturation of marketing messages, read 'Product placement: you can't escape it' at http://www.usatoday.com/money/advertising/2006-10-10-ad-nauseum-usat_x.htm

[3] Raymond Bauer and Stephen Greyser of Harvard University's Graduate School of Business Administration asked people to count the advertisements to which they paid at least some attention, finding that each day brings 76 advertisements of which a person is to some degree aware – *Advertising in America: The Consumer View*, 1964. Charles F. Adams, working with the Bauer and Greyser data in 1965, emphasised that of the 76 advertisements a day of which a person might be aware, only 12 made any kind of impression – *Common Sense in Advertising*, 1965. And a recent poll from my own agency showed that people could recall an average of 1.7 ads from the last 24 hours.

[4] Academic researchers commonly discuss the schism between creatively-focused and effectiveness-focused agency people in their papers. One such paper is 'Creativity vs Effectiveness? An Integrating Classification for Advertising' by Kover, Goldberg & James, a précis of which is available at http://www.accessmylibrary.com/article-1G1-18063239/creativity-vs-effectiveness-integrating.html

[5] This unattributed and rather premature verdict was published on p25 of the 2007 book *Power Brands: Measuring, Making, and Managing Brand Success* by McKinsey consultants Hajo Riesenbeck and Jesko Perrey.

[6] A quick calculation of the number of campaigns booked by the UK's media companies and the number of UK campaigns that win a creative award each year reveals approximately 1 in 7,000 to be creatively awarded. It's worth noting that the UK is one of the most creative advertising markets in the world, and so the figure would likely be even more weighted toward uncreative campaigns if calculated globally. 'The Link Between Creativity and Effectiveness', p7 – http://www.thinkbox.tv/upload/pdf/Creativity_and_Effectiveness_Report.pdf

[7] You can watch a really excellent series of presentations, including Tess Alps' introduction and Peter Field's 'The Link Between Creativity and Effectiveness' at http://www.thinkbox.tv/server/show/nav.1320

CHAPTER TWO

Chapter Two is an expansion on the article 'Creative = Effective', which first appeared in *Campaign Brief* magazine, January 2008

[8] 'Are Advertising Creative Awards Really Worth the Cost?' by Lisa Sanders, *Advertising Age*, 15 June, 2006. http://adage.com/article/cannes06/advertising-creative-awards-worth-cost/109918/

[9] 'Pitch Secrets: How Clients Really Think' by Martin Jones, *Campaign*, 20 March, 2009. http://www.campaignlive.co.uk/news/892385/Pitch-Secrets-clients-really-think/?DCMP=ILC-SEARCH

[10] 'Commercial Art Must Be Both' by Eric Hirshberg, *Creativity*, 25 August 2008. http://creativity-online.com/news/commercial-art-must-be-both/130130

CHAPTER THREE

[11] If you haven't read UK advertising luminary Jeremy Bullmore's column 'On the Campaign Couch' then you should. This particular quote came from the 18 September 2009 edition: http://www.campaignlive.co.uk/news/941068/Opinion-campaign-couch-JB/?DCMP=ILC-SEARCH

[12] As at February 2011, BBDO was Network of the Year at Cannes for the fourth year running, #1 Network in the Big Won Report for the fourth year running and Most Awarded Agency Network in the World in the Gunn Report for the fifth year running.

[13] 'Creative Enough for the Finance Director' by Millward Brown's Andy Farr and Sue Gardiner, *Admap*, March 2001

[14] Richard Huntington's blog, and particularly the post that this quote came from, are great. http://www.adliterate.com/archives/2008/03/the_four_is_2.html

[15] 'Ideas are just a multiplier of execution' by Derek Sivers. http://sivers.org/multiply

[16] From the blog of Dave Trott – http://www.cstadvertising.com/blog/2010/11/80-idea-80-execution/

[17] Listen to the ad at http://www.consortium.co.nz – click on the pink box seventh from the left and fourth from the top.

CHAPTER FOUR

Chapter Four is an adaptation of the articles 'We are not here to do what has already been done', which first appeared in *Idealog* magazine, January/February 2007 and can be read at http://idealog.co.nz/magazine/7/we-are-not-here-to-do-what-has-already-been-done and 'Casualties of Coincidence', which first appeared in *Idealog* magazine, July/August 2010 and can be read at http://idealog.co.nz/magazine/28/casualties-coincidence

[18] Colenso BBDO's Vodafone 'Symphonia' TVC can be seen at http://www.youtube.com/watch?v=R3nSoEhY8SM

[19] The 'Happy Christmas from AKQA' video, eerily similar to our Vodafone spot, can be seen at http://www.youtube.com/watch?v=FgBUqJzgvBo

Notes

[20] I would like to thank Maggie Antone for introducing me to Malcolm Gladwell's article 'In the air: Who Says Big Ideas Are Rare'. The article didn't make it into *What the Dog Saw*, Malcolm's collection of New Yorker articles, but it's a must-read for the Gladwell obscurist, and freely available at http://www.newyorker.com/reporting/2008/05/12/080512fa_fact_gladwell

[21] When Smith, Chen & Yang catalogued the academic research into creativity for their 2008 *Journal of Advertising* paper 'The Impact of Advertising Creativity on the Hierarchy of Effects' they found five studies that concluded that "creative ads enhance consumers' unaided recall of ad ideas", thereby showing that original advertising stands out more, both in the media landscape and later in the mind: Pick, Sweeney & Clay, 1991; McQuarrie & Mick, 1992; Stewart & Furse, 2000; Pieters, Warlop & Wedel, 2002; Till & Baack, 2005.

[22] IMDB's 'Highest Grossing Films of All Time' list evolves constantly, but each time I revisit it I find the same glut of unoriginal cinema and a dearth of truly new stories. See if that still holds true today at http://www.imdb.com/boxoffice/alltimegross?region=world-wide

[23] Like reading about the childhood of a celebrity, it's pleasantly voyeuristic to peruse the genesis of Dove's 'Campaign for Real Beauty', one of the most famous advertising efforts of the 2000s. 'The Real Truth About Beauty' is available at http://www.campaignforrealbeauty.com/uploadedfiles/dove_white_paper_final.pdf

[24] For a long time I'd had a hunch that advertising arguments lost momentum over time as people thought their way out of them, so I was delighted to find the work of social psychologists John Cacioppo and Richard Petty. They'd explored and proved the fascinating notion that people have a tendency to develop counter-arguments over time. That work was described in 'Effects of Message Repetition and Position on Cognitive Response, Recall and Persuasion' from the *Journal of Personality and Social Psychology*, volume 37, 1979.

[25] 'The Impact of Advertising Creativity on the Hierarchy of Effects' by Smith, Chen & Yang, *Journal of Advertising*, Winter 2008.

CHAPTER FIVE

[26] Thank you to Donald Gunn who generously forewent the time and cost of sending me his seminal and pre-PDF study, 'Do Award-winning Commercials Sell?', in the post. The Gunn Report people tell me it'll be more easily accessible on the internet at www.gunnreport.com from 2011.

[27] I hope that I've done 'The Link Between Creativity and Effectiveness' justice in my retelling of its story. The original and very brilliant debrief remains available at http://www.thinkbox.tv/upload/pdf/Creativity_and_Effectiveness_Report.pdf

[28] The McKinsey & Company study, 'Art Meets Science: Creative Advertising Examined', was published on p25 of their 2007 book *Power Brands: Measuring, Making, and Managing Brand Success*.

[29] vault.com, a leading career intelligence firm, periodically ranks management consulting firms according to their prestige and standing within the business community. McKinsey & Company was #1 on that list in 2011 and had held that position for six consecutive years.

CHAPTER SIX

[30] 'Breaking Through the Clutter: Benefits of Advertisement Originality and Familiarity for Brand Attention and Memory' by Pieters, Warlop & Wedel, Tilburg University, The Netherlands, published in *Management Science*, June 2002

[31] Pick, Sweeney & Clay, 1991; McQuarrie & Mick, 1992; Stewart & Furse, 2000; Pieters, Warlop & Wedel, 2002; Till & Baack, 2005.

[32] 'Recall & Persuasion: Does Creative Advertising Matter?' by Till & Baack, University of South Carolina, USA, published in *Journal of Advertising*, Fall 2005

[33] 'Beyond Attention Effects: Modeling the Persuasive and Emotional Effects of Advertising Creativity' by Yang & Smith, Universities of Wisconsin-Milwaukee and Indiana, published in *Marketing Science*, September/October 2009

CHAPTER SEVEN

Chapter Seven is an adaptation of the study 'Creative = Successful', which first appeared in NZ *Marketing* magazine, March/April 2010, under the title 'Ideas Man', and can be read at http://www.marketingmag.co.nz/magazine/2010/03/ideas-man/

[34] Volkswagen's share data are available at http://finance.yahoo.com/q?s=VOW.DE

[35] The S&P500 growth figures quoted are averages across the two years preceding the crowning of the Advertiser of the Year in question. So, for example, in the case of Volkswagen, crowned in 2009, the average S&P growth across 2007 (5.49%) and 2008 (-37%) was -15.8%.

[36] 'P&G Share Price Soars' – http://www.highbeam.com/doc/1G1-171927331.html

[37] P&G share data are available at http://finance.yahoo.com/q?s=pg

[38] Honda share data are available at http://finance.yahoo.com/q?s=HMC

[39] Honda's IPA Effectiveness Gold winning paper 'What Happened When Honda Started Asking Questions?' isn't in the public domain, but if you've got a WARC account, just search the title.

[40] adidas share data are available at http://finance.yahoo.com/q?s=ADS.DE&ql=0

[41] adidas 'Impossible is Nothing Campaign Case Study' – http://marketing-case-studies.blogspot.com/2008/01/impossible-is-nothing-campaign.html

[42] PlayStation Sales Information – http://en.wikipedia.org/wiki/PlayStation_2

[43] BMW Films Sales Information – http://en.wikipedia.org/wiki/BMW_Films

[44] BMW share data are available at http://finance.yahoo.com/q?s=BMW.DE&ql=0

[45] Nike Annual Report 2002 Chairman's Letter to Shareholders – http://media.corporate-ir.net/media_files/irol/10/100529/Areports/ar_02/letter.html

[46] Swatch share data are available at http://online.wsj.com/quotes/stock_charting.html?symbol=uhr.vx

[47] Anheuser-Busch share data are available at http://finance.yahoo.com/q?s=BUD&ql=0

[48] Sony share data are available at http://finance.yahoo.com/q?s=SNE&ql=0

[49] Here, Mr Stengel is referring to Donald Gunn's 'Do Award-winning Commercials Sell?' study – carried out at Leo Burnett during the period when Michael Conrad was Chief Creative Officer of Leo Burnett Worldwide.

[50] *How Disruption Brought Order* by Jean-Marie Dru, p214.

[51] See adidas' impressive growth through the 2000s in their 2009 Annual Report – http://adidas-group.corporate-publications.com/2009/gb/en/adidas-kompakt/ten-year-overview.html

CHAPTER EIGHT

Chapter Eight is an adaptation of the article 'The Conversation', which first appeared in *Idealog* magazine, July/August 2009 and can be read at http://idealog.co.nz/magazine/22/the-conversation

[52] 'Restaurant to Yelp Reviewers: Bring It On' – http://bits.blogs.nytimes.com/2009/03/06/restaurant-to-yelp-reviewers-bring-it-on/

[53] Daniel Yankelovich talks in detail about his exploration of corporate trust in 'The Thought Leader Interview' – http://www.strategy-business.com/article/05309?pg=all and 'Exploring business's social contract' – http://trustedadvisor.com/trustmatters/157/Who-Should-You-Trust-on-Trust-in-Business-Yankelovich-or-Fortune

54 'Trust in Governments, Corporations and Global Institutions Continues to Decline' – http://www.weforum.org/en/media/Latest%20Press%20Releases/PRESSRELEASES87

55 I must thank David Armano, whose designation 'The Conversation Economy' I've used regularly to help those around me understand the value of campaigns that create word of mouth. Read his original thought piece 'It's the Conversation Economy, Stupid' at http://www.businessweek.com/innovate/content/apr2007/id20070409_372598.htm

56 'Digital Influence Index' – http://digitalinfluence.fleishmanhillard.com/

57 'When Did We Start Trusting Strangers?' – http://www.umww.com/global/knowledge/view?Id=34

58 While writing this book I've eaten several Grapefruit and Lemon Frujus. They're a simple ice lolly but they give you a really authentic sour fruit shudder and make you twist your face up. I don't know why that's the best thing on a hot day but it is. They won't be around for much longer, but they had a brief comeback this summer thanks, in part, to the Facebook group: 'When they got rid of Grapefruit and Lemon Frujus I died a little inside' – http://www.facebook.com/group.php?gid=4699129977

59 You can watch a Comcast technician sleeping on a lady's couch at http://www.youtube.com/watch?v=CvVp7b5gzqU

60 'Coca-Cola: Drinking the World Dry' – http://www.waronwant.org/news/latest-news/15153-coca-cola-drinking-the-world-dry

61 '40% of top fifty UK brands' Google pages feature negative PR' – http://econsultancy.com/us/press-releases/8884-40-of-top-fifty-uk-brands-google-pages-feature-negative-pr

62 Web stats site compete.com shows that ford.com was visited between one million and one and a half million times over ten of the 12 months of 2010. Google AdWords' keyword tool shows that 'ford' averages 45.5 million searches a month. Nike does a little better – 4 million visits to nike.com vs 30.4 million 'nike' Google searches. Vodafone, far worse. Just 25,000 people go to Vodafone.com each month. 30 million – 1200 times as many people Google 'vodafone'.

[63] 'Consumer Technographics® 2002 North American Benchmark Study', Forrester Research

[64] "This story is absolutely true," I was told by Sarah from Method's customer service team when I called to check whether the Chinese whisper I'd heard was fact. "This was an isolated incident in which Eric, at a press interview, drank some toilet bowl cleaner to prove the safety of our products. He does not do this on a regular basis and we do not encourage consumers to ingest our cleaning products."

[65] 'Method: Progressive Domestic', *Contagious Magazine*, Issue 13, 2007

[66] 'Nomis Puts Its Right Foot Forward' – http://www.footy-boots.com/nomis-football-boots-right-boots/

[67] 'Four'N Twenty Magic Salad Plate' – http://www.effies.com.au/awards_winners.aspx?year=2009&id=3&wid=18&awardType=EFFIE

[68] 'The Yellow Treehouse' – http://www.caanz.co.nz/usr_files/file/Effies/2009/Colenso_BBDO_Yellow_Silver_and_Bronze.pdf

[69] 'Cry for Yelp' – http://www.onthemedia.org/transcripts/2009/03/20/04

CHAPTER NINE

[70] 'Drowned in Advertising Chatter: The Case for Regulating Ad Time on Television' – http://findarticles.com/p/articles/mi_qa3805/is_200604/ai_n17172414/

[71] Gallup & Robinson's May 2000 *Journal of Advertising Research* paper 'Advertising Attitudes and Advertising Effectiveness' concluded that "advertising performance is influenced by consumers' attitudes toward advertising in general. Respondents with more favourable attitudes toward advertising recalled a higher number of advertisements the day after exposure and were more persuaded by them."

Notes

72 I borrowed Heath, Nairn & Bottomley's eloquent description of metacommunication, from their paper 'How Effective is Creativity? Emotive Content in TV Advertising Does Not Increase Attention', published in the *Journal of Advertising Research*, December 2009. The original 1967 research is available in 'Pragmatics of Human Communication' by Watzlawick, Bavelas, & Jackson.

73 'Advertising Creativity Matters', Dahlén, Rosengren & Törn, published in *Journal of Advertising Research*, Vol. 48, No. 3, Sept 2008

74 'The Link Between Creativity and Effectivness', p7 – http://www.thinkbox.tv/upload/pdf/Creativity_and_Effectiveness_Report.pdf

75 The work of John Phillip Jones in the USA, Colin McDonald in the UK & Burckhard Brandes in Germany, summarised in 'Pre-testing Methods: The Agony of Choice' by Tim Broadbent, *Admap Magazine*, October 1997.

76 'Do Award-winning Commercials Sell?' – www.gunnreport.com

Images

CHAPTER ONE

Page 13   'BMX' image courtesy of Ben Couzens
Page 16   'Times Square' image by Terabass, used under Creative Commons license (http://creativecommons.org/licenses/by-sa/3.0/deed.en)

CHAPTER THREE

Page 45   'Banana' image courtesy of Wieden+Kennedy/Honda, photography by Paul Zac

CHAPTER FOUR

Page 58   'Godmarks' image by Chuck "Caveman" Coker, used under Creative Commons license (http://creativecommons.org/licenses/by-nd/2.0/)
Page 60   'Vodafone Symphonia' image courtesy of Colenso BBDO/Vodafone; 'AKQA Christmas Video' courtesy of AKQA
Page 64   'David' image by Rico Heil, used under Creative Commons license (http://creativecommons.org/licenses/by-sa/3.0/deed.en); 'Hermes' image by Roccuz, used under Creative Commons license (http://creativecommons.org/licenses/by-sa/2.5/it/deed.en)
Page 69   'Backstreet Boys' image by Anirudh Koul, used under Creative Commons license (http://creativecommons.org/licenses/by/2.0/deed.en)
Page 72   'Campaign for Real Beauty' image courtesy of Ogilvy/Unilever

CHAPTER SIX

Page 102   'Bill Bernbach' image courtesy of Matt Whetherly (mwhetherly.daportfolio.com / mwhetherly@live.co.uk)

CHAPTER EIGHT

Page 130   'Workers at Pizzeria Delfina' image courtesy of Pizzeria Delfina
Page 140   'Susan Boyle' image by Deborah Wilbanks, used under Creative Commons license (http://creativecommons.org/licenses/by-sa/3.0/deed.en)
Page 144   'Lil' Bowl Blue' image courtesy of Method. Creative Director of Packaging: Sally Clarke, VP of Industrial Design: Josh Handy
Page 146   'Magic Salad Plate' image courtesy of Clemenger BBDO/Four n' Twenty
Page 148   'Yellow Treehouse' image courtesy of Pacific Environments Architects, photo by Lucy Gauntlett

CHAPTER NINE

Page 158   'St Francis of Assisi' painting by Francisco de Zurbarán, c.1658

Acknowledgements

Thank you to everybody who helped make this book happen:

Scott Bedbury, Ashley Bellview, Simon Bird, Tim Broadbent, Michael Conrad, Ben Couzens, Nick Cullen, Tony Davidson, Peter Field, Nick Garrett, Donald Gunn, Vincent Heeringa, Olivia Johnson, David Lubars, Michael Lynch, Jim McDowell, James McGrath, Jim Moser, Huw O'Connor, Paul Rees-Jones, Terry Savage, Fred Senn, Jim Stengel, Bruce Tait, Joe Thomson, Suresh Vittal, Scott Wallace, Matt Whetherly and Emma Wilkie.

A huge debt of gratitude to Colenso BBDO Studio Legend Shayna Armstrong for her tireless work wearing out her Mac to knock this thing into shape.

Also to the team at Tangible Media – Vincent Heeringa, Martin Bell and Matt Cooney for their support over the years, and Ali Jacobs for her production talent and grace.

To those people who've been my most inspiring creative teachers and partners during my years in advertising – Josh

Moore, Paul McElwain, David Thomason, Brent Smart and Nick Worthington.

And finally to my beloved wife Annabel and our children Tripp and Harper. If ever there were a case for creativity...

About the Author

James Hurman is Planning Director at New Zealand advertising agency Colenso BBDO.

One of the world's most creative agencies, Colenso BBDO was named New Zealand Agency of the Decade for the 2000s by Campaign Brief magazine, and is part of the BBDO network, named network of the year by the Cannes International Advertising Festival, the Gunn Report and the Big Won report for several years running.

Colenso BBDO has been recognised more for its effectiveness than any New Zealand agency, winning several local and international Effectiveness Agency of the Year and Effectiveness Best in Show awards in recent years.

James was selected for the inaugural Cannes Creative Effectiveness Lions jury, is Chairman of the 2011 and 2012 New Zealand Effies, is a regular contributor to *Idealog*, New Zealand's premier business magazine and teaches strategic thinking at Auckland University of Technology.

He can be contacted at thecaseforcreativity.com